IDENTITY
THEFT
in CANADA

Outrageous Tales & Prevention Strategies

Lisa Wojna

QUAGMIRE PRESS

IDENTITY THEFT
in CANADA

Outrageous Tales & Prevention Strategies

Lisa Wojna

QUAGMIRE PRESS

The Publisher: Quagmire Press Ltd.

Library and Archives Canada Cataloguing in Publication

Wojna, Lisa, 1962–
      Identity theft in Canada: outrageous tales & prevention strategies / Lisa Wojna.

Includes bibliographical references.
ISBN 978-1-926695-20-4

      1. Identity theft—Canada. 2. Fraud—Canada. I. Title.

HV6685.C3W64 2012   364.16'330971   C2012-903251-4

Project Director: Hank Boer
Project Editor: Kathy van Denderen
Cover Images: foreground figure © Andrea Danti / Shutterstock; binary background © cg artist / Shutterstock

Produced with the assistance of the Government of Alberta, **Government of Alberta** ■
Alberta Multimedia Development Fund

PC: 1

Contents

Dedication

~

To J.B., S.A.A. and L.A.A.—three tiny treasures who must learn early how important it is to be careful, but not paranoid, in this life and to still view the world with innocent wonder.

~

Acknowledgements

~

Writing this book was a little like running through a labyrinth. Just when I thought I'd found a path that was going to lead me to a particular destination, I was sidetracked into another topic. This of course led to many starts and stops and forays along forked byways until I began to question where I started and had to retrace my steps to the beginning. I must therefore begin this book by emphasizing how the product you see here is largely the result of the keen sensitivity and sharp eye of an amazing editor, Kathy van Denderen, who is as talented as she was patient. Thank you for taking my good intentions and often-unwieldy prose and packaging it into a clear and concise document.

Thank you to my publisher, Quagmire Press, for trusting me to write about this important topic. Thank you to my dear friend and mentor, Faye. Your friendship and advice is valued beyond words. And thank you to Taylor Printing in Wetaskiwin for doing quick print jobs for me in between far more lucrative projects so I could meet my deadline.

I also owe an endless debt of gratitude to the many journalists, writers and other authorities who have followed the cases and issues discussed here in the pages of their respective newspapers or publications. I am also indebted to the producers, directors and broadcasters of various newscasts and documentaries as well as to the voices of brave victims who have shared their stories with the media. My additional thanks to the Royal Canadian Mounted Police, Canada's various municipal police forces, the Canadian

Anti-Fraud Centre and all the other advisory watchdogs that this country is so lucky to have.

The most important advice these organizations promote is that education is the key to protecting ourselves from identity theft and identity fraud. This book echoes that sentiment. It is my hope that what follows in these pages provides you, the reader, with a better understanding of identity theft and its related frauds, as well as some tools to help you protect yourself from these types of crime. And should you be unfortunate enough to become a victim of identity theft or fraud, I hope the information will provide you with the help you need or guide you in the right direction to recover your good name and peace of mind.

Thank you to my longsuffering family without whom this book and anything else I attempt would be meaningless. And a special thank you to my darling Jada who, once again, had to share her mommy with the computer and chose to add to the kitchen-table clutter with projects of her own so we could be together. I love you, baby.

Introduction

~

In 2012, the RCMP launched its Fraud Prevention Month campaign, held each year in March, with a press release that led with the following statistic:

Fraud-related offences are now thought to be as profitable as drug-related offences, estimated at between $10 and $30 billion annually in Canada by the RCMP's Commercial Crime Branch.... Fraud should concern all Canadians because it destabilizes our national economy while strengthening organized crime groups. The impact on individuals, families and businesses is devastating: retirement savings, homes, businesses—and in some cases, lives—have been lost.

It's a frightening statement that can't help but make a reader stop and take notice. While there's admittedly a distinction between some types of fraud and identity theft, the two crimes are linked more often than you might think. The unauthorized use of your bank or credit card to withdraw cash or pay for something is not only financial fraud but is also a fraud that is perpetrated by a form of identity theft. Someone has impersonated you, if only for a moment, a day or for many years on and off, and the financial fraud committed in your name began with the theft of your identity.

Because incidents of identity theft and its ensuing identity fraud are often shrouded in embarrassment, where victims mistakenly believe they were foolish and should not have fallen for a particular offer or scheme in the first place, law enforcement agencies in this country have stated publicly that it's difficult to create a statistical picture of exactly how many Canadians have been victimized by this crime. However, the Department of Justice did go on record upholding information culled through a November 2006 Ipsos-Reid survey. According to the information collected, "73 percent of Canadians are concerned about becoming victims of identity theft, and 28 percent say they or someone they know has already been a victim of identity theft."

In 2010, new surveys suggested both concern about identity theft and that the number of people who'd fallen victim to this crime had increased dramatically: the Canadian Anti-Fraud Centre reported 18,146 known identity fraud victims lost an estimated $9.4 million that year alone. And in February 2012, Equifax Canada released an article stating the information compiled from its "fraud solution database for the financial sector reveal that there was more than $650 million in fraud incidents detected across Canada in 2011."

Clearly, identity theft and identity fraud are a growing threat in today's society—a threat that isn't about to disappear overnight, if ever. And if you are unfortunate enough to fall victim to identity theft and fraud, the U.S. Federal Trade Commission states that, on average, it takes almost a full year before victims even notice the crime had been committed—and a lot longer than that to rectify the problem.

So where are you vulnerable? And how can you protect yourself from having your identity impersonated and becoming a victim of fraud?

The first step is to acknowledge that this very personal crime exists. If you need proof, turn to your local media—identity theft and identity fraud are hot topics these days, with new stories head-lining almost weekly. A CBC News item coming out of the metro Vancouver area on March 20, 2012, is a case in point. Police raided a residence in Burnaby and seized "various computers, stolen mail, passports and a range of tools used to make fake documents." They also uncovered "44,000 IDs, 80,000 stolen credit cards, hotel receipts from the Surrey Sandman and Kingsway Ramada, a Canada Post bag and numerous weapons." Police verified that false accounts had been opened in "virtually every chartered bank," and that, according to Inspector Tim Shields, was merely the tip of the iceberg. The items in this seizure represent almost every type of identity fraud you can name, and there's no telling what further damage would have resulted had these culprits not been apprehended.

While the BC example sounds as though it originated from a television drama, felons are working 24/7 in neighbourhoods like the ones we live in, devising ways to strip you of your good name and use it to further their illegal schemes.

The sad reality of our society is that just about everything we do can open us up to this kind of attack. If you have a bank account, carry a credit card, receive snail mail, open emails, scan the Internet, use a cellphone, drive a vehicle, pay a mortgage, have a utility in your name—all of which provide a certain ease to our lives—you leave yourself open to unscrupulous folks who can appropriate the information for their benefit.

Education is the best weapon we have when it comes to combating any of life's difficulties, and identity theft and fraud are no exception. As the RCMP stress in their annual campaign, "The only good news is that the majority of frauds can be prevented by identifying the methods used by fraudsters. The more you know about a fraud, the less likely you are to fall for it."

This book is all about learning to identify the areas where criminals can gain access into our lives, and it suggests ways to protect against identity theft and identity fraud at home, in the workplace, online, with our finances, on social media networks, and more. I will review the various scams that have historically drained victims' bank accounts and how to spot new scams and recognize how they're all merely new twists on an old theme—it's those new twists that pull in unsuspecting victims.

As the Canadian Anti-Fraud Centre says, "There is no reason to be paranoid; there's just reason to be careful. If someone wants desperately to target you, they can probably get a lot of information about you—so you just need to minimize the criminal's opportunities to get that information. You can make yourself a harder target and that is the best defense."

Since I first started the journey of writing this book, many of my personal practices have changed. I've become far more cautious about the mail I toss into the garbage, making doubly sure my name and address aren't on any of the envelopes—most utility bills are addressed on the actual bill, with the address showing through an envelope window, so I recycle those envelopes. I shred or burn all receipts. I'm careful about the amount of information I give out to a telephone solicitor or how I answer the questions I'm asked when I call my banking institution or credit card company about my account. And I've spent a considerable amount of time deleting "friends" from my Facebook list who I don't personally know.

I don't take these precautions because I'm paranoid…but you never know when you might cross paths with someone desperate for a new identity.

One caution to readers: this book is presented to you as information. The topic of identity fraud is as quick to change as the tempting emails and conniving telephone calls that daily barrage us, so don't stop here. Use the suggestions found in these pages to protect yourself, but also keep your ears and eyes open for new updates from the media, and be smart in all your interactions. Consider this book a hand guide and journal, jotting new facts or sources in the margins of these pages for added reference.

Be on guard and stay aware in whatever you do, but stop short of becoming paranoid. Take precautions with your personal business, but don't let the criminal actions of the few make you jaded.

~

Chapter One

What Is Identity?: An Overview of the Many Complicated Definitions

~

Without getting too philosophical, "identity" is commonly defined as "the individual characteristics by which a person or thing is recognized." The personal, physical, philosophical, psychological and spiritual components that come together to define each of us are unique. Historically, we have placed a great deal of value on our personal identity. And with every successive generation, parents have charged their offspring with the responsibility of upholding their family's honour and warned of the shame that would befall them if anyone disgraced the family's good name.

As with anything dear or precious, your name is a treasure to possess. And as with any other treasure, your name could become the object of someone else's desire. Whether an individual is simply discontented with his or her life or is in a difficult personal situation, donning an assumed identity might present itself as the only escape from a bad circumstance. It's seen as a way to get a fresh start on life.

Besides, the idea of remaking oneself into someone else isn't just a logical option; as it happens, assuming a different identity is a fairly simple process.

A MORAL DILEMMA?

In 1993, 20th Century Fox released *Mrs. Doubtfire,* a movie that critics of the day argued was the funniest film to ever hit the big screen to that point in the history of American cinematography.

Based on a novel by British writer Anne Fine, the tale of Mrs. Doubtfire centres on a family struggling with the demise of a marriage. Daniel Hillard (played by Robin Williams), an unemployed but devoted father of three, finds himself cut off from his children following a difficult breakup and custody dispute. Devastated, he connives a desperate way to maintain contact with his children (and ex-wife)—he takes on the persona of Mrs. Doubtfire and lands himself a job as the children's nanny.

The comedy tracks Hillard's antics and the challenges he faces while assuming the identity of Mrs. Doubtfire and how he surprisingly manages to fool his ex-wife and children. There is no arguing the comic value of the movie, and as the viewer you can almost buy Hillard's disguise and imagine how you could pull off a similar ruse if you were living this man's life. In fact, most viewers can empathize so completely with Hillard's character and his unfortunate circumstances that they might even defend his actions despite the questionable morals.

Assuming a false identity is a theme that has presented interesting twists in literature throughout the ages. But fiction is often based on fact, and disguising oneself as another person—or even the opposite sex—isn't as unbelievable as the fictitious Mrs. Doubtfire might lead us to believe.

Take the fairly recent case of Bernard Boursicot, whose story was immortalized in the 1988 classic play by David Henry Hwang, *M. Butterfly*.

Boursicot, a 20-year-old French diplomat posted at the French Embassy in Peking, first met the Chinese opera singer Shi Pei Pu in 1964. Sparks flew between the young man and the 26-year-old entertainer, and before long, Boursicot's affection for the star grew so powerful that it pulled the sexually inexperienced Boursicot into a full-blown affair that lasted nearly two decades.

In the intervening years between 1964 and 1979, Boursicot and Shi Pei Pu drifted apart. It was a tumultuous time in China—some historians suggest that in 1966, Mao Tse-tung launched the "greatest revolutionary movement" the world had ever seen. The Great Proletarian Cultural Revolution lasted 10 long years, and the politics between the Chinese and the rest of the world made it difficult for Boursicot to visit the object of his affection. Desperate to see his lover, the young diplomat passed more than 100 classified documents to Shi, allegedly to secure his lover's personal safety and maintain contact with her.

The political upheaval of the day caused such a strain that finally, in 1979, Boursicot and Shi lost touch with one another. It was a temporary estrangement: in 1982 the couple managed to reconnect when Boursicot smuggled Shi, and the son Boursicot believed he had sired during his affair with Shi, out of China. The couple settled in Paris and, for a short time, they continued to live in seeming bliss.

The clincher to the story is that even though the couple was purportedly intimate, and Shi had earlier claimed to be pregnant and produced the son Boursicot called his own, the "woman" of Boursicot's dreams was, unbeknownst to the diplomat, actually a man.

Remarkably, Boursicot claimed he didn't know Shi Pei Pu was a man until the couple was arrested for allegedly "spying for China" in 1983. When the authorities told Boursicot his lover was a man, Boursicot demanded to see for himself—he wanted to view Shi's naked body standing before him. And although both men were incarcerated at the time, that's exactly what happened. When faced with the reality that the woman of his dreams was a man, Boursicot fell into a deep depression. During his time in jail he attempted suicide.

This story, with all its twists and turns and forays into espionage, is no doubt one of the most bizarre tales of someone assuming a fake identity, but transgendered identity theft is by no means unique to this scenario. At various points throughout history, and still today in some cultures, young girls have passed themselves off as boys to avoid being raped or to enable them to acquire an education that, in their place and time in history, was only available to males. Women have also impersonated men in order to infiltrate military operations, to find long-lost family members, to travel alone when it wasn't possible for them to do so, or to acquire better jobs.

While one can't negate the compelling reasons why some individuals might be driven to use another identity as a means of survival, this book examines the criminal components involved with assuming someone's identity for personal gain. Taking another person's name and reputation as your own is a deception of monumental magnitude, and as Alfred Hitchcock put it, deception of any kind weaves a tangled web that can't help but ensnare anyone walking through its path. Someone always gets hurt when the truth is circumvented, and the injured party is most often an innocent bystander.

But what if the name you assume is fictional, like Mrs. Doubtfire? Maybe you've simply used a last name out of the telephone book, picked a new first name from a baby name book and paid someone to fabricate your driver's licence and passport after reading a "how to build a new identity" website. If the new name you assume isn't pulled out of your neighbour's mailbox or collected by any of the other numerous ways an identity thief might fish for new victims, does anyone get hurt?

PUTTING A NAME TO THE CRIME

According to the *Oxford English Dictionary*, the term "identity theft" was first coined in 1964. The term, or some rendition of it, has been around for decades now, but identity theft wasn't something the general public knew much about until fairly recently, unless of course they had their identity stolen or knew someone who did. And for years, the authorities were in many cases equally in the dark about what at first appeared to be a fairly rare crime.

Even when the authorities finally put a name to the crime, they have haggled over its definition because stealing someone's identity is rarely a means to an end; identity theft is almost always connected, in some way, to other criminal activities. Once obtained, a false identity can be used to do more than merely start one's life over with a clean slate. A fake name can garner a criminal with all sorts of financial benefits, help land a good job, access health care on someone else's dime, acquire a mortgage or conceal illicit activities by muddying the waters of an investigation.

There are also different degrees of identity theft—or at least degrees with which someone's identity can be misappropriated. Identity theft can be as simple as a criminal using another person's name to gain access to that individual's credit card or bank account information and make unauthorized transactions. Instead of assuming a single individual's identity on a permanent basis, this brand of opportunist looks for ways to bilk large numbers of people out of as much money as possible. Financial institutions have tagged this kind of theft as "payment card fraud," and it's this micro-distinction that has further complicated the topic for the public and law enforcement officials alike.

With that in mind, some authorities argue the term "identity theft" is a misnomer of sorts because no one can actually steal an identity, as the term suggests. Instead, "identity fraud" provides a more accurate description of what's really going on when someone's identity has been appropriated because doing this typically precludes some manner of fraudulent behaviour.

The RCMP Commercial Crime Branch (CCB) defines identity theft as "the preparatory stage of acquiring and collecting someone else's personal information for criminal purposes." Identity fraud is "the actual deceptive use of the identity information of another person (living or dead) in connection with various frauds (including for example personating another person and the misuse of debit card or credit card data)." Both terms are often used interchangeably, but the RCMP CCB prefers to use the term "identity fraud" over "identity theft" because "the vast majority of crimes committed using personal information without authorization involve fraud."

For the purpose of this book, I will use a broad stroke in defining the terms "identity theft" and "identity fraud" as "stealing an individual's identity for the purpose of furthering one's own agenda in any way, especially financially." Additionally, I will explore fraud in general and mass-marketing fraud (MMF) specifically because of its large scope and its association with ID crimes. As the Canadian Anti-Fraud Centre (CAFC) states, "often MMF involves identity crime, which includes identity theft and identity fraud."

A LOOK AT THE NUMBERS

As of the writing of this book, the most recent statistics released by the CAFC, which was originally founded in 1993 to deal with the ramifications of mass-marketing schemes, state that the total number of identity-theft complaints processed between January 1 and December 31, 2011, more than quadrupled the number of complaints processed in 2010. Because the CAFC distinguishes between identity theft and identity fraud to gain a better understanding of the issues, separate numbers are kept on identity fraud, although the connection between the two crimes is still reinforced. According to CAFC's findings, the number of identity-fraud complaints in 2011 was slightly lower than in 2010, but the dollar value attributed to those complaints was significantly higher in 2011.

The CAFC closely monitors mass-marketing fraud and its various components. The number of mass-marketing fraud complaints was only slightly higher in 2011 than those received in 2010, but again, the dollar value attributed to this fraud was several million dollars higher in 2011. Here's the breakdown as it was available in the spring of 2012:

- In 2011, the total number of identity-theft complaints received was 4687, compared with 965 in 2010.

- In 2011, the dollar value attributed to identity fraud as reported to the CAFC was $13,214,563.61, compared with $9,603,281.54 in 2010.

- According to CAFC's 2010 annual report, reports of mass-marketing fraud had been filed from every province and territory, but the majority of complaints (about 17,000) come from Ontario residents.

These numbers by themselves are disturbing, but they are even more telling when you take into account that the CAFC estimates that the numbers they collect, and the total dollar loss attributed to those numbers, represents "less than five percent of the total number of victims overall." In other words, most victims never officially report their experiences.

Equifax is an American-based company that manages "consumer and commercial data," including personal credit reporting. Additional statistics from its Canadian branch in a February 2012 news release suggest further dismal findings when it comes to the financial cost of identity theft and fraud:

- There were $650 million worth of Canadian fraud incidents reported in 2011. Of that number, "13 percent of the total number of fraud incidents" made up the bulk of money lost, accounting for more than $400 million.

- "$1.7 million of attempted fraud activity was detected daily."

- Personal bank and credit card accounts totalled more than $225 million in losses of which $160 million was attributed to fraudulent loan applications, another $48 million connected with personal bank deposit accounts and an additional $17 million to credit card fraud.

- While credit card fraud accounted for only three percent of the total dollar losses in 2011, it actually "accounted for more than 40 percent of the total number of incidents detected."

- The lowest incidents of fraud were recorded in November and December (perhaps the con artists were caught up in the seasonal festivities).

- April and May recorded the highest incidents of fraud (see the section on mail fraud for more information on this subject).

PROTECTING YOUR PRIVACY

So exactly how do the private details of your life become vulnerable to someone planning to steal your identity with fraud in mind?

In a 2007 report on identity fraud in Canada compiled by the RCMP's national Criminal Intelligence Program, "even the simplest criminal is computer smart. Many have laptops with templates for numerous types of I.D. from multiple provinces." This is why new versions of debit cards, credit cards and driver's licences are embedded with chip technology—it makes it harder for criminals to duplicate them.

All that identity thieves, or identity fraudsters, need to do is collect a handful of facts on an individual and they are well on the way to extorting someone's identity and using that information for their own purposes. The felons often store complete victim profiles on their computers to use when they need it, which might include sharing your vital statistics with other offenders or organized criminal groups. Their techniques are often quite crude, and that lack of sophistication reinforces how easy it is for a criminal to steal the personal information of Canadians, wherever they are located. To safeguard your privacy, and inevitably your identity, it's important to recognize that it's not just some anonymous computer junkie holed away in a dark room conniving ways to attack thousands of unprotected computers by creating mock websites and badly written spam that you have to concern yourself with. Sometimes the culprit is a lot closer to home.

In 2003, a Federal Trades Commission study revealed that in the U.S., more than 25 percent of all identity-theft victims knew the thief who targeted them. In "35 percent of those cases, the thief is a family member or a relative." While nationwide statistics in Canada don't clearly define these kinds of statistics, it's reasonable to believe we'd get a similar result.

Our work colleagues can also pose a threat to identity theft. Just as we do in our homes, we expect a certain amount of safety in the workplace. We believe that the personal documents we leave on our desks or on our computers are secure and that a mutual respect for privacy will ensure that a workmate won't rifle through them. But unfortunately, this is a naïve point of view. The RCMP Commercial Crime Branch warns that corrupt employees in the workplace pose a real threat to theft involving personal information.

And given the right set of circumstances, absolutely anyone could become a victim of identity theft or identity fraud.

Basically, because you have a name, you can become a target. You don't even need to have a heartbeat to fall victim to identity theft and its resulting frauds—obituary columns, war records, missing persons records from natural disasters and names from headstones provide endless fodder for people seeking a fake identity. Personnel records accessed through large businesses, old high school yearbooks, newspaper articles and social media websites represent but a handful of the many places where thieves can access the information necessary to steal someone's identity.

Thieves might be even more direct. They might have been scouting you in particular and know where you live. Perhaps they have picked up your mail without your knowledge and then hoofed it over to a registry office in a neighbouring community to apply for a new birth certificate or photo identification.

Identity thieves have been known to use the name of a deceased individual and acquire the services of a lawyer to obtain a birth certificate. The writer of one website chock full of "how-to" information on identity theft, shared how one of his friends, who was trying to acquire a new identity by using the name of a deceased individual, pulled off his ruse. In this case, the man in question told a lawyer that he was "looking for a missing heir and needed to see the potential heir's birth certificate." The lawyer, who was new to that community, charged a fee in advance and within 30 minutes was able to present his client with "a certified copy of the birth certificate he wanted, [and] copies of both the individual's parents' birth certificates too." Although this incident occurred in the U.S. (clients in Canada have to wait for birth certificates to arrive in the mail), the point remains the same and shows how shockingly easy it is to request and acquire a "replacement" birth certificate. If the U.S. system contains holes, you better believe Canada has holes too. In addition, residents of both countries are able to exploit these loopholes in their neighbouring nations—identity thieves don't let a little thing like national boundaries limit their efforts.

Even young children aren't exempt from the threat of having their identity stolen. They're especially vulnerable because they're not consumers and obviously don't have a credit history to keep tabs on. That means the young victim wouldn't know if someone had applied for a credit card using the child's name until later in life when the child is an adult and applies for credit. At that time, the victim's identity would have been compromised by an identity thief who reneged on the bills.

The threat of child-related identity theft is much higher in the U.S. because newborns usually receive a Social Security Number shortly after their birth. But even in Canada, with the prerequisite of children acquiring a Social Insurance Number (SIN) before their parents can participate in investment opportunities such as the Alberta Centennial Education Savings Grant (ACES) and the Canada Learning Bond, it's not uncommon for a child to have a SIN at a young age. An identity thief only needs a name and a SIN, or some other form of identification, and he or she can do a lot of damage— a youngster's credit rating can be run into the ground long before that child is old enough to apply for credit. And as unbelievable as this next tidbit of news is, the U.S. Federal Trades Commission notes that family members steal the identities of the minor children in their families to obtain credit they wouldn't otherwise be able to get. It is a disturbing and growing trend in identity theft. And you can bet that if it's happening in the U.S., it's happening in Canada as well.

News Alert:
Worse Than Taking Candy from a Baby

Identity thieves targeting Canadian children made headlines in June 2011 with CBC reports about a man who pleaded guilty to stealing the identities of deceased children to pad his wallet.

Dean Turner admitted to recording the names of children from gravestones in New Brunswick graveyards and using the names to apply for SIN cards, birth certificates and ultimately Old Age Security benefits. According to the news clip, Turner resurrected the identities of 11 dead people. Among those victims was a 10-year-old girl who passed away in 1932 and another was a "two-day-old boy who died in 1968."

The concept seems absolutely unbelievable, and yet Turner managed to collect $17,000 by stealing the identity of one of those deceased individuals before he had his day in court.

According to the RCMP CCB, the following list represents some of the ways your personal information can be acquired:

• Corrupt co-workers keep a mental log of the information you share verbally, or they outright sift through your personal papers when you're not at your desk.

- Close friends, family members or roommates may have access to your personal information and/or financial documents.

- Strangers or acquaintances break into residences, vehicles and businesses.

- Fraudulent mass marketers try to gain your trust to access your wallet.

- Internet-savvy criminals phish (use the Internet to illegally gain confidential information) or pharm (lure unsuspecting victims to fraudulent websites for the same purpose as phishing) by spamming email boxes with messages connected to harmful spyware or malware and then are able to gain unauthorized access to your computer.

- Fraudulent websites threaten your computer with viruses and Trojans.

- Strangers dumpster dive or rifle through your garbage for personal and financial information.

- Individuals steal your snail mail for similar documents.

- Thieves lift your wallet, purse or briefcase.

- Individuals access social networking sites looking for your personal information.

Once someone has your personal information, he or she can do all kinds of damage to your personal finances and good credit rating. Here are some of the ways identity theft and fraud can be used against you:

- Unauthorized use of debit and credit cards

- Access, open or close bank accounts or acquire loans in your name

- Forge cheques

- Mortgage or title fraud which, as defined by the Canadian Intelligence Service Canada, is "the deliberate use of mis-statements, misrepresentations or omissions to fund, purchase or secure a loan...[or] any scheme designed to obtain mortgage financing under false pretences, such as using fraudulent or stolen identification or falsifying income statements"

- Use your personal information to make a false insurance claim

- Fraudulently acquire government documentation

- Fraudulently access government programs, services and benefits

- Immigrate to Canada or emigrate from Canada under false pretences

- Acquire utility services and cellphone accounts using your name and information

- Election fraud—the altering or misrepresentation of election votes

The pursuit of identity theft and its subsequent fraudulent interactions are big business in the criminal world, which, as I previously alluded to, is a world that knows no geographic boundaries. Because the criminal activities that stem from the false impersonation of one individual by another are seemingly endless, people involved in identity fraud usually have a background in many other illicit activities as well. Therefore, the RCMP have suggested identity fraud has been linked to several criminal groups in Canada, including but not limited to:

- Asian organized crime

- West and East African criminal networks

- Sri Lankan–based groups

- Pakistani-based groups

- Middle Eastern–based criminal groups

- More than 300 street gangs in operation across this country

INSIDE THE MIND OF THE IDENTIFICATION THIEF

Profiling identity thieves is considerably more complex than the encapsulated version of criminal psychology espoused by prime time television dramas such as *CSI* and *Criminal Minds* might suggest. Identity thieves might work alone, with a partner or as part of a much larger network. They might be looking for ways to turn a quick profit, assume an identity to hide from law enforcement or simply want to disappear from their current life.

It's remarkably easy to assume another name—just ask Google. Are you in desperate need of a second chance at life? According to one website, if you are living a woeful existence, the only way to wipe the slate of your life clean is to acquire a new identity. "These days more people than ever are changing identity," the website claims. "They're seeking to change identity because they know it's the only real effective way to walk away from their past problems."

This particular self-proclaimed authority is pumping up the value of its new, updated 2012 ebook on how to "Plan your total

disappearance" by "legally" acquiring a "new or 2nd driver's license—
Legally create a clean new credit record—Perform a SECRET name
change...Change your social security number." The site also offers
online sources where individuals can obtain "legal fake passports"
and information on the best towns to move to where "no one asks
questions." This all begs the question, of course, of how one can
acquire a "legal fake" document and why it would be necessary to live
in a town where "no one asks questions" if this process is indeed completely "legal" in the first place?

The same site promoting its "legal" options uses Ferdinand
Waldo Demara as an example of one of the techniques it supports
for acquiring a new identity. Demara, it argues, successfully used the
"ghosting method" of striking out for a second chance at life; ghosting is "a form of identity theft whereby an individual assumes the
identity of a deceased individual." As endearing as Demara was said
to be by most people who knew him, this "famous" individual, who
as the site pointed out, was the subject of the movie *The Great
Imposter*, was a master identity thief. No matter how loudly he
claimed he did not injure anyone during his exploits or how clearly
he defended himself by pointing out all the good work he did under
the several personas he assumed, Demara left victims in his wake.
And not every identity he stole was that of a deceased person. The
doctor he impersonated wasn't too happy to have an uneducated
man use his name to practise medicine, in the navy nonetheless, and
perform surgery on soldiers who relied on him to have expertise he
did not legally possess. Demara might have been smart and person-
able, but it was nothing short of a miracle that someone didn't die
because of his deceit.

As was mentioned earlier, any form of identity theft, even if the perpetrator claims the theft occurred simply to "remake oneself," results in fraudulent behaviour. Moreover, most instances of assumed identity are contrived for something a little darker than a second chance at life.

But if you're going to the extent of remaking yourself, anxious that your deceit remains unknown to those around you, building a fictitious character out of nothing more than a name has its own set of risk factors. Referring back to the above "how-to" website authority, when it comes to effectively assuming a new identity, it's a lot easier—and more effective in the long run—to steal the identity of a real person, living or dead, than it is to create a fictitious ID from scratch. To begin with, anyone wanting to perform a background check on you for personal or professional reasons will no doubt have a lot of unanswered questions if the person you claim to be goes no deeper than a name selected from an online name generator. Imagine, as this website suggests, a future father-in-law doing a background check on his daughter's fiancé and coming up with no back story—it leaves far too many questions unanswered. The website goes on to say, "This is why people who want to change their identity, do so by looking for a good one to assume."

Regardless the reason why someone would choose to assume a false identity, for the one in six Canadians who have fallen victim to identity theft, the ensuing injury caused by this crime can take away years from a person's life and requires thousands of dollars to repair. In some cases, the extensive harm left in the wake of this crime has cost the victim his or her life—a 2002 U.S. Senate committee report on the effects of identity theft on the elderly included testimony about a Florida senior who fell into such a deep depression after her identity was stolen that she committed suicide.

THE LONE WOLF

Ever hear the saying that if you are speaking to a friend in public, there are often as many as six other pairs of ears overhearing your conversation? Most of these eavesdroppers might only pick up on a portion of what you're saying because they're not particularly interested in listening. However, some eavesdroppers are standing nearby and paying close attention because they are on the lookout for a new opportunity.

This kind of stand-alone fraudster is often referred to as a lone wolf. Lone wolves aren't interested in acquiring a new identity to "start over." They're interested in making money, plain and simple. The lone wolf is somewhat of a hermit by nature, prefers to work alone, has an alpha personality and is continually looking for new ways to score. The lone wolf is usually multi-talented, not afraid to work hard and get dirty and can conjure up any number of ideas on how to turn a quick buck. And while a lone wolf works independently, a pack's worth of them can be wandering about at any given time.

You need to be wary of lone wolves.

GETTING DOWN AND DIRTY

It's common knowledge that one man's trash is another man's treasure, especially when it comes to lone wolves and crumpled receipts or old and faded credit card slips. For these dumpster divers, discarded scraps of paper are diamonds in the rough that need nothing more than a little polishing to show their shine.

Dumpster diving is one of the oldest means by which scammers and identity thieves can tap into some of your personal information and make money for themselves at your expense. It was admittedly easier to make money this way many years ago, with the old manual-swipe credit card machines that left an imprint of your entire credit card number on each of the three copies of the receipt. When electronic credit card machines required customers to swipe their card, or more recently insert a card with a chip, the complex technology made it more difficult for fraudsters to gather the information they were looking for.

It became more complicated, but not impossible.

For one thing, not every store, kiosk or home-based business can afford to change over to new technology as soon as it arrives. There is a natural period of transition, which not only informs criminals a change is about to take place but also gives them time to work on new ways to get the information they want—while still exploiting the businesses that are slower to get on board with new methods. Even today, years after swipe machines have been installed in major box stores and months after chip technology was introduced, countless merchants still aren't using the new swipe or chip technology. It's simply not economical for small, independent businesses, such as farmers' market merchants and crafters, to put out the cash required to set themselves up with the new payment system. Instead, if they do accept credit card payments for their goods, they're probably still using a manual-swipe machine or perhaps even writing your credit card number onto your receipt. That means your entire number is there for anyone to recover should you toss your receipt in the trash. If a thief retrieves these numbers, he or she can gain control of your credit card in any number of ways. And even with the businesses that have changed over, there are still machines that print out the entire 16-digit credit card or debit card number on customer receipts instead of only the last few digits of that number.

Admittedly, this whole dumpster-diving idea is a hard way to make a living. You might argue it would be easier to get a real job rather than scamming innocent people by digging through trash cans and picking sales receipts from coffee grounds and mouldy pasta sauce. The smell itself, never mind the mess, makes me wonder what possible appeal dumpster diving might hold as far as employment options go. And now, with more and more merchants accepting electronic payments, there's no guarantee that a lone wolf will find an entire credit card or debit card number for all the dirty work.

No problem. There is more than one method of scamming a credit card—and this one comes without the mess and stench.

PIN PAD THEFT

In a perfect world, inputting your information on a merchant's debit or credit card machine would be safe. The appropriate amount of money is withdrawn to pay for your purchase, and that would be the end of the transaction. But there are risks with everything. While most merchants are honest and wouldn't ever think to retrieve the sensitive personal information you've input into their machine for their financial benefit, an unscrupulous employee might not think twice about "accidentally" dropping your card on the floor so he or she can record your card number and then watch you punch in your Personal Identification Number (PIN) so they can later empty your bank account. Crooked clerks wearing miniature cameras have an edge when it comes to getting both PIN information as well as bank card numbers, and strategically placed video surveillance cameras have provided some unsavoury employees with an eagle-eye view of customers for the same reason.

Then there's the outright and brazen theft of the PIN pads themselves, which are loaded with personal customer information that can provide fraud artists with a potential gold mine. As it turns out, it's quite simple to make a PIN pad disappear and replace it without anyone knowing.

When it comes to PIN pad theft, criminals will quite often work in pairs, approaching a retail outlet toward the end of the business day. These criminals are banking on empty stores and tired employees who want to get home after spending their workday fielding customer requests. So when a customer rushes into the store right before lockup, asking for one more thing, the tired clerks are quick to comply—the sooner they can satisfy the customer's request, the sooner they can lock up and go home.

In this scenario, an accomplice might distract a clerk while his or her partner takes aim at disarming and stealing one of the cashier's PIN pads, leaving a decoy PIN pad in its place. When the decoy is secured and the original PIN pad is in the accomplice's pocket, the pair leaves the store to complete their plan. Once they're back home, they install the mechanisms necessary to record customer debit and credit card numbers and their corresponding PIN numbers. The next day, the pair will return to the store and replace the decoy PIN pad with the original. Now, all they have to do is wait a day or two.

According to public information articles provided by the Edmonton Police Service, the criminals involved in the initial PIN pad theft will eventually return to the store again, only this time they don't need to enter the premises. They can sit in the comfort of their vehicle and download all the information swiped and punched into the PIN pad since the time that the alterations were made "remotely via a Bluetooth modem."

Once the criminal's memory chip is filled with information, the data is downloaded and transferred onto blank, magnetically stripped cards. The next step is a visit to the nearest ATM (Automated Teller Machine) to make as many withdrawals as possible. Because the victims would not have noticed anything out of the ordinary during the shopping trip where their cards were scanned, it could take several days before they realize their bank accounts have been emptied or credit card limits maxed.

The victims of credit and debit card theft have not only been robbed, but they have also had their identity impersonated, their credit record potentially damaged and their resources significantly depleted while the criminals involved in the scheme lined their pockets and got away without detection. Depending on how long it takes for the targeted retail outlet to catch on to what has happened, the video surveillance of the night the PIN pad was originally switched might no longer exist, having been erased and reused, giving the criminals a get-out-of-jail-free card.

Scenarios such as the one described above have propelled PIN pad manufacturers and distributors and the businesses they serve to work together to secure more sophisticated procedures to combat crime. Steel mounts were devised to fasten the pads to cashier counters, while still keeping within requirements for disabled people. Installing upgraded cable clips and locks with tamper-evident labels are additional features that allow retailers and their employees to notice if a PIN pad had been tampered with. Prior to these security measures, removing a PIN pad from a cashier counter was remarkably straightforward—the connection between the device and the register was similar to the way a telephone cable clips into the wall, or a modem cable secures onto a computer. Businesses that do not use steel mounts are still susceptible to PIN pad theft—and a lot of businesses have yet to put the money into upgrading their security features.

It makes you wonder how safe it is to pay for your restaurant meal with a hand-held PIN pad.

News Alert:
Technology No Barrier for Determined Identity Fraudsters

Thieves made a brazen attempt at stealing PIN pads at several Toronto-area Tim Hortons locations on January 9, 2012. The two male suspects used wire cutters to snip the keypads at the drive-thru windows at five different locations before the police apprehended them at the Tim Hortons drive-thru on the corner of Kingston and Markham roads.

CBC News reported that the men in custody placed

an order at each of these drive-through windows and told the clerk they were paying by debit.

"Once the debit card machine was handed to the customer, they would cut the cord of it and drive away with the PIN pad," Toronto police detective Shawn Mahoney told reporters. The pair was charged with a total of 48 offences.

In late January and early February 2012, Durham, Toronto and York police forces, along with the RCMP, joined forces in arresting 12 individuals suspected in belonging to a debit-card-skimming fraud ring responsible for stealing more than $300,000 and compromising as many as 280 ATMs, "as well as pay-at-the-pump machines at several gas stations."

Toronto Sun reporter Terry Davidson reported that among the items seized in an eight-warrant investigation was "equipment allegedly used to copy debit-card information at bank machines and gas station ATMS...[along with] equipment used to forge credit cards... fraudulent cards, $40,000 in cash, computer equipment and three high-end vehicles...."

Another story coming out of the Greater Toronto Area on February 28, 2012, created headlines like the one in the *National Post*: "Toronto Police Lay 357 Charges in Alleged ATM-tampering Scam." This time the communities of Toronto, Pickering and Brampton were targeted by what police believed was a ring of seven people who trafficked much of the items and information they stole from more than 1500 credit-card holders to customers "all over the world, from Europe to South Africa."

While chip technology makes it difficult for criminals to duplicate debit cards, not all countries use cards with chips. As Ian Nichol, a representative of the Toronto Police's financial crimes unit, pointed out to reporters, when our neighbours to the south don't use chip technology it makes it easier for fraud artists to duplicate cards and empty bank accounts.

Also in January 2012, a similar story came out of Edmonton, where investigators believed a dozen people were responsible for skimming a half a million dollars from 900 bank accounts. Once again, the account numbers were collected from fraudulent PIN pads, and at the time this story hit the *Edmonton Sun*, investigators suggested many other accounts might have been compromised but not yet accessed.

With countless photographs on hand connecting several individuals to the Edmonton fraud case, investigators with the city's economic crimes unit issued warrants for 10 of the 12 suspects. As of the writing of this book, police were still working on identifying the other two individuals they believed were involved in this gang of thieves that appeared to be "highly organized" and "very careful" but didn't necessarily have one particular leader.

According to Edmonton Police Service (EPS) Constable Elvin Toy, this specific case covers a larger geographic area than the city of Edmonton; investigators believed Montréal was the group's home base. Toy also referred to these fugitives as "travelling criminals" who "often changed their appearance with moustaches, beards, [and] hats." These factors made it more difficult to positively identify the suspects and track their activities. Extensive co-operation between police forces in both cities and the RCMP is necessary in order to capture the suspects—24-year-old Giscard Grand-Pierre, the first of 10 suspects eventually arrested in this case, was apprehended in Montréal on January 11, 2012.

Investigators were also examining the possibility that one or more of the suspects were involved in a similar Edmonton-area scam that took place in 2010 and included "four organized card-skimming operations."

To date, both the above cases were still before the courts.

WIRELESS IDENTITY THEFT

The ease with which criminals could steal credit card information increased significantly when some of the world's major banking institutions recently introduced "wave" cards—credit cards you don't need to insert or swipe but instead wave in front of a reader. This new technology opened the door to tech-savvy fraudsters with even the smallest amount of money to invest in their craft. These criminals no longer had to worry about wading through stinky garbage or taking the risks involved in stealing and doctoring PIN pads. Something like abbreviated receipts was not a stumbling block to their scamming schemes. They found another way to piggyback on new technology—to ride the wave, as it were. They discovered that by tweaking the mechanics behind a small machine known as a Radio Frequency Identification (RFID) reader, they could get all the information they needed without ever raising the slightest suspicion.

PC Magazine defines RFID as "a data collection technology that uses electronic tags for storing data. The tag…is made up of an RFID chip attached to an antenna. Transmitting in the kilohertz, megahertz and gigahertz ranges, tags may be battery-powered or derive their power from the RF waves coming from the reader."

The magazine outlines the similarity between RFID tags, which are as small as a grain of rice, and bar codes—both are used for identification purposes. The main difference is that bar codes must be near a scanner or "reader" to collect information while "RFID tags do not require line of sight and can be embedded within packages."

This isn't a new science. In fact, one source pointed out that RFID technology was "first used in World War II to identify friendly aircraft." But the technology sat on the backburner for several decades and only re-emerged in the 1970s and '80s. That's when innovative manufacturers such as the automotive industry started exploring ways RFID knowledge could be used to improve their products. Since then, RFID technology has continued to evolve. In March 2012, *RFID Journal* reported that RFID cards and readers were being used to "link shoppers' activities with their Facebook accounts, enabling the marketing of events, businesses or products, and providing users with discounts and other offers." Other associated wireless technology was being utilized in hospital settings to "automate the testing of emergency lighting, measure the length of cardiopulmonary emergencies, record temperature levels and detect water leaks."

RFID technology clearly has benefits. So in the first decade of this new millennium, when financial institutions and credit companies started exploring the idea of embedding RFID tags into their cards in an effort to "promote a new touch-free payment system," the concept seemed like a natural evolution of the technology. Customers only needed to wave their credit cards near a payment terminal in order to pay for their purchases. One safety consideration that sounded beneficial to customers was that by using this method of payment, they didn't have to pass their card to the cashier, thereby keeping it in their possession at all times and reducing the risk of the number being scanned in some way. At least this was true for small purchases, as the wave option could only be used for purchases under $50.

It sounded like a quick and safe convenience for shoppers. Retailers and participating credit card companies also benefitted from the technology. Customers with wave cards were using them more often because of the ease and speed the RFID option offered for small purchases, such as buying lunch during a busy workday or filling a vehicle with gas when in a hurry. One article suggested customers were using their cards as much as 25 percent more each month, which was also great news for credit card companies.

But as with any other advancement in technology, there are opportunities to use it for malicious purposes, and it wasn't long before fraud artists uncovered ways to exploit the wave technology.

It was frighteningly simple, really. Retailers had to have a RFID reader to collect the information on RFID-tagged items and credit cards alike, and all a criminal had to do was obtain one of these machines. And despite new readers running into the thousands of dollars, second-hand readers can be acquired for considerably less—a 2006 *New York Times* article claimed the computer and radio components necessary to make a reading device from scratch would cost as little as $150, while a 2010 CBC report suggested one could be bought for around $10. Moreover, anyone can buy an RFID reader. And if the device gets in the wrong hands, a criminal could use these hand-held gadgets to read and scan hundreds of credit cards in a busy shopping mall or any place where crowds of people congregate without the victims knowing they'd been targeted. As University of Massachusetts researcher Tom Heydt-Benjamin told *New York Times* reporter John Schwartz in 2006, the flaws in the technology at that time were as revealing as if you were "wearing your name, your credit card number and your card expiration date on your T-shirt...."

Credit card companies loudly disputed these claims in 2006. In the same *New York Times* article, MasterCard executive Art Krazley countered Heydt-Benjamin's and his fellow researchers' claims by saying they had used a "small sample" when conducting their research. "This is almost akin to somebody standing up in the theater and yelling, 'Fire!' because somebody lit a cigarette."

In 2008, the media was still questioning the problems with RFID-equipped credit cards. It was a subject that intrigued Adam Savage and Jamie Hyneman, along with their team of researchers at the popular Discovery Channel show *MythBusters*. But when they planned to run an episode on RFID tags, they came up against some major roadblocks.

"I'm not sure how much of this story I'm allowed to tell, but I'll tell you what I know," Savage told a gathering of about 3000 people at the 2008 HOPE conference—a biannual conference put on by the Hackers On Planet Earth, an organization that has been around since 1994 and was designed to enlighten the public on issues surrounding hacking. Savage explained that he and his colleagues were planning to research the RFID topic, covering issues such as reliability and safety surrounding that technology.

"One of our researchers called up Texas Instruments and they arranged a conference call...to talk about the technology," Savage said. At the pre-arranged time, researchers from *MythBusters* and Texas Instruments connected via telephone, along with "chief legal counsel from American Express, VISA, Discover, and everybody else, and I get chills just as I describe it. They...absolutely made it really clear to Discovery that they [Discovery] were not going to air this episode talking about how hackable this stuff was."

The Discovery Channel, reliant on revenue from advertising dollars to provide programming, backed down.

The credit card companies using RFID technology continued to defend themselves, claiming their cards were safe and that the information collected in each individual transaction was encrypted. But two years later, in June 2010, the CBC released a news story that once again disputed these claims. In an investigative report by Zach Dubinsky, Seattle-based security expert Eric Johanson provided a chilling demonstration on how vulnerable these cards actually were. Johanson was able to pull a credit card number and expiry date from an unsuspecting hotel patron in downtown Toronto using nothing more than "his laptop, a PayPass reader and some software."

"When you go to read a card, you just take a reader and say, 'Give me your card number,' and it will do that," Johanson told Dubinsky. "It's still very much transmitted over the air by the RFID interface. There's no message for the card to authenticate the reader it's about to talk to—it will talk to anyone."

The credit card officials featured in the CBC story acknowledged that their wave cards did not encrypt or "disguise the card number and expiry date when they send data over the air to a card reader." RFID readers were able to procure a cardholder's name even from cards distributed before 2010, when the story came out. And while some critics argued the cards had to be within inches of the reader for information to be scanned, the readers could be adjusted to collect data from a greater distance. As with doctored PIN pads and the information they could retrieve, the data collected by an

RFID reader can be downloaded and then transferred onto any card with a blank magnetic strip.

As recently as December 2011, news reports were still emerging in the media that warned the public about RFID, also referred to as smart cards or paypass cards. Companies such as Visa Canada, Scotiabank, TD and the Royal Bank, all of whom offer this smart card technology, have repeatedly addressed these concerns by saying that so far, no one has reported having their personal information swiped and abused. However, Gord Jamieson, Visa Canada's director of risk management and security, admitted to reporter Stefania Moretti in early 2011 that "There is a remote risk that data could be intercepted but we have multiple layers of security that really address that potential, limited risk."

Additionally, according to the Canadian Bankers Association, "Visa, MasterCard and American Express have zero liability policies for unauthorized transactions. Customers are protected when using credit cards issued by banks and are not responsible for fraudulent transactions made on their cards." If you notice a security breach and report it immediately, you shouldn't have to pay for unauthorized transactions. Still, once a breach of privacy occurs, such as someone stealing your banking information and using it for his or her own benefit, the victim is left with a lengthy, time-consuming and at times expensive procedure to rectify the damage.

Technology continues to evolve, and with the media acting as public watchdogs on the issue of protecting the safety of our personal and financial information, security measures will hopefully continue to improve over time. The new smart cards embedded with chips are supposed to be more difficult to crack than the RFID technology once claimed to be. But as we have seen, nothing is foolproof. And in order to offer additional protection for consumers, some companies have claimed to come up with ways to protect bank and credit cards—and any other cards containing similar personal information. "Smart Card Defender Sleeves," advertised on the Internet and TV, promise to block RFID signals from reading the chips on your cards. Of course, as with anything you intend to purchase, check out the authority and research the item to ensure the product is indeed what it claims to be and not merely another scam.

Concerns surrounding RFID technology and leaking of personal information don't stop with credit and debit cards. New Canadian passports will now contain "an embedded contactless computer chip and antenna using radio frequency identification (RFID) technology with a frequency of 13.56 MHz." With this technology, an "ePassport reader can scan the data from Canadian passports." This reader "energizes the chip circuitry by wirelessly emanating power and communicating through its antenna." Could criminals eventually develop a technology that captures personal identification from these varieties of RFID documents? Passport Canada stands by its new technology:

> *An ePassport without chip copy protection could potentially be cloned by an impersonator with a substituted chip. This is an insignificant issue since the existing physical passport security features and passive authentication protect the ePassport against tampering.*

> *As a preventative measure to detect cloning, active authentication (AA) is implemented in ePassports. AA works by including*

a cryptographic key pair unique to each chip. While the AA
public key is digitally signed with the rest of the ePassport data
using passive authentication, the corresponding AA private key
is stored in secure memory and cannot be read or copied. During ePassport validation, the chip then proves knowledge of this
private key by means of a challenge-response protocol. This
means that the chip's private key signs a random challenge presented by the ePassport reader, and the ePassport reader then
uses the chip's AA public key to verify the signed response and
recognize the ePassport as genuine.

Passport Canada's assertion is comforting, but as with any new technology, you have to wonder how soon some missing link will be discovered and exploited and whether our personal information will be made even more vulnerable.

RETAILER RESPONSIBILITIES: WHAT HAPPENS WHEN BUSINESSES GET CARELESS

RFID readers might pose a problem to the security of customer information, but when a security breach happens on a large scale, the potential fallout is mind-numbing.

On January 17, 2007, TJX Companies Incorporated, the world's "leading off-price retailer of apparel and home fashions" and the parent company of Winners and HomeSense, announced to its customers that it had become a "victim of an unauthorized computer systems intrusion." Three months into the investigation of that breach, which revealed how hackers managed to access the financial data collected during sales transactions and identified some of the key players involved in that scam, the number of customers affected were estimated at 45.7 million worldwide. The final numbers later indicated that more than 94 million credit and debit cards were exposed, making the data breach the largest of its kind to date. Along with financial data, investigators discovered that more than 450,000 customers also had other personal information downloaded by the perpetrators, including American social security numbers and driver's licence numbers—330 of the driver's licence numbers belonged to Canadian victims.

A week later, on January 26, the clothing retailer Club Monaco announced to the media that customer credit information might have been compromised in their 28 Canadian outlets.

But retailers aren't the only businesses that have found themselves trying to repair security leaks that put our personal information at risk of exploitation. Also on January 26, 2007, a CBC news report announced that the Canadian Imperial Bank of Commerce (CIBC) had "lost a file containing the confidential information of almost a half-million Talvest Mutual Funds clients." The bank faced criticism from federal authorities because they didn't announce the loss to their clients—something the Canadian Privacy Commission encourages businesses to do. And the CIBC isn't isolated in their experience; other banks have had similar security glitches. Equifax Canada, a leader in the field of business and consumer information and technology, fell victim to a computer hacker when 2000 of their computer files were stolen in 2005. The theft was identified during a "routine security audit" in December of that year.

So what can we expect from the businesses that have required us to share our personal information for one reason or another?

The Office of the Privacy Commissioner developed the Personal Information Protection and Electronic Documents Act, which received Royal Assent on April 13, 2000, to help safeguard Canadians. In the intervening years since its inception, the Privacy Commissioner has also maintained information for retailers on how to privacy-proof their businesses. While Alberta, British Columbia and Québec have provincially regulated laws in this regard, it's safe to say there are similarities in the suggested methods of requesting personal information, and how that information is used and protected. In a nutshell, you as a consumer have the right to expect:

- Accountability from the business you are dealing with

- To be told why specific information is necessary in your business dealings

- To know if the business you are dealing with plans to share your personal information with any other business

- To be asked only what is necessary to ensure you are who you claim to be

- To have your information only used for the particular transaction you are tending to at any given time unless you explicitly agree otherwise

- That your personal information is "complete, accurate and current"

- That the organization or company you've shared that information with has adequate safeguards in place to protect your privacy

- That the organization or company you're dealing with has their privacy policies available at all times to the public

- That you can access your personal information at any time

- That you have a means with which you can challenge a company's compliance to the privacy principles

In addition, while a business can ask a customer for identification to protect against fraud, that information is not supposed to be recorded "unless the information is clearly needed for the product or service" being purchased. For example, if you are renting a vehicle, the rental company has the right to record your driver's licence information. The same is not true for a retail clerk checking your ID before accepting a credit card payment.

And the only time you need to provide your Social Insurance Number (SIN) is when an employer requires it for income-reporting purposes. SINs are not required for credit checks and should not be used as identification.

Retail outlets often request customer postal codes or phone numbers to collect demographic data for their records. You can share this information if a business explains exactly how that information will be used. However, if you are uncomfortable in giving out the information, you should know that it is not a requirement. Clerks usually have a "dummy number" they can use if a customer is reluctant to give out that information.

Some retailers might ask for personal details to help speed the process of future transactions. They cannot use that information to "track purchases" and "market products." And a business "cannot ask for the information for one purpose and then use it for another."

Regardless how small a business is, if you want to see its privacy policy, it is incumbent on that business to provide one.

Also, each business must designate an employee as a privacy officer, whose role is to make sure the company complies with the law.

Your personal information always belongs to you. Therefore, you can access and make changes to that data at any time. Businesses are required to protect customer details with the following safeguards:

- Personal Information is contained in password-protected computers

- Credit card slips are safely locked away

- Any paper files containing personal information are put in a secure place and only made available to the employees that need to access that information

- None of your personal information is ever copied

- When it's no longer needed, your records will be disposed of in a responsible manner

If you or someone you know believes they have a dispute to file regarding the use of their personal information by a particular business, contact the branch office of the Privacy Commissioner in your area. Contact information for provincial and territorial offices are listed in the Appendix of this book.

Credit and Debit Card Safety Checklist

- Take precautions to ensure someone isn't looking over your shoulder when you use an ATM or a PIN pad.

- Never write your PIN on your debit or credit card. And as with any other password, change your PIN a minimum of twice a year.

- Under no circumstances should you share your PIN with anyone, not even a family member or a banking official.

- Do not carry all of your banking and credit cards in your purse or wallet—take only the cards you need for any particular outing.

- Limit the number of credit cards issued to your name—the rule of thumb is to have no more than two major credit cards.

- Do not shove your unused credit and bank cards under your mattress or store them in a corner of your underwear drawer. Consider purchasing a small safe or using a safe-deposit box for cards that you only use occasionally, such as during a vacation.

- If you shop online, use a credit card with a low limit of $500 or $1000.

- Make a list of your credit card numbers and expiration dates, bank account numbers and bill due dates and keep the list in a safe place. New replacement credit cards typically arrive a few weeks before the previous ones expire. Contact your credit card company to find out their usual procedure and then watch for your new credit card in the mail. If it doesn't arrive when expected, contact the company.

- Similarly, personal activation numbers for some major credit cards are mailed within a week or two of the arrival of your new credit card. Check your mail daily, and again, if the number doesn't arrive when expected, contact your credit card company. Receiving your credit card mail late, or not receiving it at all, could indicate that someone has been monitoring your snail mail and has intercepted your mail.

- If your credit card bill is expected in the mail, check your mailbox to ensure you've received it on time. If a credit card statement doesn't arrive when expected, telephone your credit card company to make sure the bill hasn't been lifted from your mailbox.

- Always check each item on your credit card statement to ensure that nobody else has made a charge to your credit card.

- If you use Internet banking, do not wait until you receive your statement in the mail or online. Instead, check your banking and credit account information weekly. If your accounts have been compromised, it is imperative you maintain due diligence and report the fraudulent activity immediately. A delay in reporting can result in you being held responsible for that financial loss.

- Change your online passwords regularly, and always use some type of letter-number combination that contains at least eight characters.

- Cross-shred all financial statements and receipts after verifying the charges—some credit card receipts still have a full credit card number on them, and it isn't uncommon for dumpster divers to reconstruct statements and receipts that have gone through a regular shredder. Therefore, it's important to use a shredder that shreds documents in a criss-cross fashion, making it harder for dumpster divers to piece together documents.

- T4 forms, mortgage statements, and receipts and statements for tax returns seven years and older can be destroyed. Cross-shred all of these items. (Note: the legal requirements relating to keeping important documents frequently change. When you are given the green light to destroy these documents, they should all be cross-shredded.)

- Cross-shred any mail that offers you a pre-approved credit card. Throwing these letters away without doing so makes it quite easy for someone to retrieve the form from the trash and return it to the credit card company with a "change of address" to redirect the forthcoming card to the fraud artist.

- Cross-shred credit cheques that some major credit card companies send out on occasion, and instruct the company to refrain from sending these cheques to you. In many cases, your entire account information and personal details are contained on these cheques and, if they fall into the wrong hands, can easily result in identity theft or fraud.

- Check your credit regularly. For a nominal fee, you can have a company monitor your credit and alert you to any new activities on your credit report file on a monthly basis. At the very least, check your credit at one of the major credit reporting agencies once a year.

- Be cautious about where you use your debit and credit cards. Some individuals use plastic almost without exception, but there is an argument to be had for using cash when making a purchase at a business that is unfamiliar to you.

- Be aware of where you use your credit cards. This will help you cross-check your monthly statements.

- When making a purchase, keep an eye on your card at all times. Whenever possible, do not hand over your card to the cashier.

- Don't use your credit or debit card on a machine that isn't secured to the counter. If the business hasn't put this simple safety measure in place, consider going to your nearest ATM to withdraw the cash you need and returning to make your purchase.

- Whether you're buying groceries or gas or withdrawing money from an ATM, never leave without your receipt, and do not toss it into the nearby wastebasket, even if you tear it up beforehand. Persistent criminals won't balk at piecing together torn receipts.

- Think twice before paying for your restaurant meal on a hand-held PIN pad. Again, paying with cash is a safer payment option.

- Pay attention to your surroundings. If you are travelling in a crowded area, make note of being shoved or bumped into for no apparent reason. Busy locations are a gold mine for criminals with RFID readers.

- Consider approaching your banking institution for information on credit card protectors, also known as RFID-scan blocking sleeves. One source suggests wrapping your bank and credit cards in tin foil, claiming the metal prevents a RFID scanner from reading the card information. There are also special wallets on the market that claim the same protection for your cards.

- Never give out your credit card information online or over the telephone unless you've initiated the transaction. This means, of course, that you have determined the website or the merchant you are dealing with is trustworthy in the first place and has installed adequate security measures so your information won't be compromised.

- Never send sensitive information via email. That includes credit card and bank account details, as well as Social Insurance Numbers, driver's licence numbers, insurance information and so on—email correspondence is vulnerable to hackers.

- And finally, the Financial Consumer Agency of Canada offers a great tip—if you routinely use a laptop at work or school, never leave it unattended or unlocked. The same holds true for personal digital assistants (PDAs), cellphones, iPods, iPads and other electronic devices: all of these items can contain your personal information.

Chapter Two

Identity Fraud: Victim Profiles

~

WHAT'S YOUR STATUS?

I f you don't take some of the precautions mentioned in Chapter One, you might not find out until it's too late to garner the financial protection promised by banks and credit card companies.

That's what happened to BC residents Mark Gorst and Shannon Werry.

The couple's nightmare began in 2007 when they noticed large withdrawals made electronically from Gorst's Royal Bank of Canada (RBC) account. After further investigation, Gorst learned that his ex-roommate had been added to his bank account, which enabled the individual to transfer money from Gorst's account to their own.

Gorst reported the fraud to the RCMP but was told the problem was a bank matter. But discussing the situation with his bank didn't resolve Gorst's problem because it had been more than a year since the "initial crime" had occurred. The length of time that had elapsed meant his banking institution wouldn't cover his loss.

This initial discovery was only the first of many assaults when it came to Gorst's identity fraud troubles. Shortly after his discovery, Gorst discovered he wasn't receiving direct deposits for his tax refunds and GST cheques, and more than $20,000 in credit card debts had been racked up to cards issued to his name—cards that he hadn't applied for and didn't own. He was being inundated with telephone calls from collection agencies, and furthermore, the alleged fraudster was trying to cash large cheques with a forged signature.

"I have no credit," Gorst told CBC News in September 2009. "I have nothing in my name. I can't own anything, because it could be seized by creditors."

Gorst is on the hook by the banks and credit card companies for the $20,000 in credit card debt because too much time had passed between the time when the debts were made and reported. Gorst and Werry said they knew who was behind Gorst's ruined credit rating and mountain of debt—and that they could prove it. The couple taped a telephone conversation that incriminated the individual in an effort to back their claims to the authorities. However, when the CBC article was penned, Crown counsel hadn't approved the charges the RCMP believed they were able to file on the case.

"It's frustrating…because you know who it is—and you have the proof that you need—and nothing happens," Gorst told reporters, adding that the statute of limitations had expired with the two-year delay between the time most of his money was stolen and when Gorst noticed the theft. And what makes matters worse is that Gorst once knew and trusted the individual who was now causing him so many problems.

"I made the mistake of leaving my ID and my mail on a bed-room counter or kitchen counter where anyone could have grabbed it—and someone did," Gorst said.

Most of us would agree that it's unfair that Gorst is left with a financial mess he didn't produce and with the responsibility to clean it up in order to regain his once-stellar credit rating. Like Gorst, most Canadians don't check their credit rating unless they apply for credit in the first place. And if Gorst hadn't noticed the money being siphoned from his bank account, which alerted him that something was up, he too may not have learned about the credit card debt attached to his name until he actually applied for credit. Scenarios like the one Gorst found himself wading through are becoming more commonplace, and the authorities are racing to edu-cate the public about the dangers of identity theft and identity fraud and the methods we can adopt to protect ourselves.

Law enforcement is also trying to change how the law deals with victims and perpetrators of identity theft. In 2009, when Gorst had talked to CBC reporters about his situation, Canada's Criminal Code did not list identity theft and fraud as a crime. As of January 8, 2010, that changed when Senate Bill S-4 became law, "making it illegal to possess another person's identity information for criminal purposes."

However, this new law doesn't change the circumstances of people like Gorst.

So how do you know if you've been a victim of identity theft? Here are a few situations from the Canadian Anti-Fraud Centre that could tip you off that someone is impersonating you for their own financial gain:

- You discover that someone has conducted a credit check on your name when you are contacted by a creditor you haven't previously conducted business with.

- You receive mail or telephone calls from a company saying you've been denied or accepted for credit that you hadn't applied for.

- You start receiving bills for a credit card you did not apply for or that you don't possess.

- You start receiving bills for items you haven't purchased.

- A creditor contacts you stating you haven't paid your bills, or you start receiving calls from collection agencies about accounts you do not have or purchases you did not make.

- You notice the usual credit card bills you receive through the mail haven't arrived in some time. Even if you haven't used your credit card during a particular month, it's imperative you look for your bill and check it to ensure your credit information hasn't been compromised.

FRAUD VICTIM PROFILE:
JANICE GOOFERS

It was well past the supper hour when 24-year-old Janice Goofers finally pulled into the driveway of her home on January 27, 2010. The Alberta resident worked as an educational assistant at a local school, a career that she supplemented with a second job at a local nursing home. It had been a long day of working with high-energy students and although it was only 8:00 PM, Janice was tired. The sun had set hours ago, adding to the exhaustion Janice felt, and she was more than ready to call it an early night.

Shutting off the engine of her '95 Chevy truck, Janice reached across the seat to grab the few groceries she'd picked up at her local Safeway, along with as many of the various and sundry items she'd dumped into the truck throughout the day. She grabbed her keys last and, unable to lock the truck doors because the locks were broken, simply shut the workday behind her with the thrust of the driver's door.

It wasn't until the next morning that Janice noticed something was missing. She was dressed and ready for work, lunch was packed and she had her keys in hand. But where was her wallet?

At first, Janice wasn't overly worried. Thinking back to the last time she used her wallet, she knew she'd had it with her at Safeway when she paid for her groceries the previous night. Most likely she'd forgotten the wallet in her truck in her rush to carry her bags into the house, she surmised. Locking the front door behind her, Janice hurried to her truck to still her nerves—she didn't have much time before she needed to be at school.

That's when the full impact of her situation revealed itself: the wallet was not in the truck. Janice was now sure she had left her flat, purple billfold on the truck dashboard. That's where she always left it, but it wasn't there now. She was overcome with a wave of nausea as she began to realize what must have happened. Janice knew that if she couldn't find the wallet in the house, and it wasn't in the truck even though she remembered placing it on her dashboard, then someone must have stolen her wallet from her unlocked truck.

Convinced of her conclusions, Janice called the school to say she'd be late for work. She knew she needed to file a report with the Leduc RCMP, but before she did that she wanted to make a few phone calls. Along with all of her personal identification, Janice had a debit and credit card in her wallet, and she wanted to make sure no one could access these accounts.

She was about to find out that while she was unwinding from her long day at work, someone had already been using her cards and had put a healthy dent into her finances.

Each police or RCMP station may have a slightly different variation to the type of paperwork or exact procedure followed when reporting what, at this point in Janice's story, was a theft of property. Janice filled out a witness statement at 9:25 AM on January 28, providing the RCMP with all her personal details and a brief description of what had occurred.

Janice's statement was simple because there really wasn't a lot to elaborate on. She remembered putting her wallet on her dashboard around 8:00 PM on January 27, and by 8:00 AM the next day, when Janice got into her truck to go to work, the wallet was gone. Although she didn't carry cash, her wallet contained her debit and Visa card, as well as her driver's insurance and registration papers, her birth certificate, SIN card, Alberta Health Care card and some retail club cards.

"Have any of the cards been used?" asked the officer taking her statement.

With the few calls Janice had made before heading to the RCMP detachment, she learned that the person who had stolen her wallet had used her Visa card twice: once at a St. Albert Trail 7-Eleven gas station for the sum of $221 and a second time at the St. Albert Walmart for a staggering $957.42. Both those transactions took place within two hours of Janice arriving home with her groceries. In less than 24 hours, Janice's credit card balance had increased by almost $1200.

Janice was now not only the victim of the theft of a wallet, but through the unauthorized transactions on her credit card, she was also technically a victim of identity theft.

In a 2012 identity theft prevention campaign, British Columbia RCMP suggest that one way to know you've become a victim of identity theft is when an unauthorized payment has been charged to one of your accounts. Janice was lucky that she took such quick, decisive action in reporting the theft of her wallet and contacting the financial institutions she dealt with. Her rapid response ensured the fraudulent charges were covered by the banking institutions involved and they didn't rely on her for payment.

At the same time, Janice had a lot more to worry about than the unauthorized use of her credit card. With the amount of personal information the thief collected in stealing Janice's wallet, the culprit could open new bank or credit accounts in Janice's name and leave her to foot the bill—and the thief in this case made several attempts at doing just that.

As well as the direct financial damage, the woman responsible for this crime could have used Janice's identity in other ways. She could have applied for welfare, employment insurance or other government programs. Worse still, the thief could have used Janice's identification to hide out from the police or other officials who might be looking for her in connection with another crime or perhaps used Janice's ID in the commission of a new crime. The thief could have supplied Janice's identification to larger criminal groups looking for ways to illegally bring people into Canada. Or the thief could have applied for a mortgage in Janice's name and used that new home to start up a marijuana grow operation or methamphetamine lab—not as far-fetched an idea as it may sound. (Mortgage fraud is discussed in detail in an upcoming chapter.)

In the months and years following the theft of Janice's wallet, several credit cards were applied for in her name. At one point, the thief changed the PIN for Janice's debit card—a process that is actually a lot easier to do than you would think possible. Once that PIN was changed, the identity thief cashed a bogus $2390 cheque and then withdrew the $1000 maximum allowed prior to the mandatory five-day hold most banks put on personal cheques to ensure they clear.

And in February 2012, almost two years after the initial theft of Janice's wallet, she is still feeling the ramifications of her identity theft. After purchasing a new cellphone, her account was frozen because the authorities wanted to make sure it was actually Janice opening the new account and not someone impersonating her. Janice was left without a telephone for more than a week—a minor inconvenience when compared to what could happen if the safeguards Janice put in place weren't working and someone else applied for that account. Still, it's an inconvenience she wouldn't have had to endure if she wasn't victimized that cold January night in 2010.

Janice never discovered the identity of the woman who stole her wallet and used her identity, on and off, in the two years since that fateful day. Video surveillance footage at one bank showed a pixillated image of a woman using Janice's personal information to cash a cheque. The culprit was clearly a woman who bore no resemblance to Janice, but the picture wasn't clear enough for anyone to provide a positive identification.

Janice looks back on her experience with mixed feelings. She's grateful that her situation was rectified as quickly as it was, but she has lost the earlier innocence she once had about life and the people around her.

FRAUD VICTIM PROFILE: PATRICK GUEST

A sense of disillusionment is only one of the many emotions an identity-theft victim experiences when struggling to emerge from this kind of nightmare. On average, it takes a victim a year of consistent work to erase the stains of identity theft. But for Patrick Guest, a resident of Kitchener, Ontario, a lost wallet and the ensuing repeated attempts at identity theft took him more than 20 years to erase.

Although identity theft has always been a concern of law enforcement, in 1990 the general public wasn't aware of how easy it was for someone to steal an identity or how damaging it could be on someone's good name. So when 23-year-old Guest had his wallet stolen from an Ajax gym, his biggest worry was replacing his ID—it did not occur to him that a stranger would assume his character.

As the weeks and months went by, any concern Guest may have had about what had become of his personal papers dissipated altogether. At least it had until he received a bill for $200 from the

Oshawa General Hospital two years later. Guest, who claimed he'd never been to Oshawa to that point in his life, had allegedly been treated at the hospital for a neck injury. The bill he received in the mail was for a neck brace he was apparently supplied with. Not long after that incident, Guest also learned his identity was being used by someone wanting to claim a disability pension.

By now Guest started to realize that the information from his stolen wallet was providing someone else with a false identity, and he called the local police to report his suspicions. But the response Guest received to his phone call was not what he had expected. Instead of showing a little sympathy and offering to help the frustrated man, the police wanted to arrest him for an assortment of offences Guest had not committed, including driving under the influence and driving without insurance.

Guest must have breathed a sigh of relief when the Durham Regional Police informed him that they had arrested Gilbert Landry in connection with the above-mentioned charges in 1993. But Guest's headaches were far from over.

It took Guest more than a year to clear the mountain of parking tickets Landry allegedly wracked up in Guest's name.

"To get them squashed, I had to submit an affidavit—in person—to each courthouse," Guest told *Toronto Star* reporter Emily Jackson in September 2011. Each courtroom visit meant Guest had to take time off work. He also had to appear in front of a justice of the peace and explain his situation. And although he managed to get all the charges dropped, Guest estimated it cost him about $2000 to clear his name.

At this point you might think Guest's nightmare was finally over. But his case proved to be an exception to that likelihood.

Twenty years later, in 2010, Guest began receiving calls from various credit card companies, asking him details about his account activities. According to the creditors, he was wracking up thousands of dollars worth of debt to fast food outlets. The sudden change of habit made them suspicious. One credit card company called to ask Guest for details on the changes to his billing address, even though Guest had not moved. Guest also received queries about a credit card he had never applied for.

To counteract what Guest now recognized as another case of stolen identity, he contacted Equifax and TransUnion, requesting they acquire his prior approval for all credit applications they might receive in his name.

It took more than a year to fix the problem. As fate would have it, it looked like the now 52-year-old Landry was once again responsible for Guest's nightmare. Durham Regional Police spokesperson David Selby told reporters that it looked like Landry had used Guest's identity "a few times over the 19-year-span" between the time Guest first had his wallet stolen and his most recent encounter with Landry's alleged fraud.

Landry ended up facing several charges, including the possession of "identity information with inference a Fraudulent Offence was Intended," "Personation to Gain Advantage" and four counts of the possession of a "credit card obtained by crime."

Guest's experience with identity theft shows how far people may have to go to clear their name once an identity thief has muddied it to the degree the thief had in Guest's case. Over the time Guest's nightmare evolved, he not only contacted the appropriate credit reporting agencies and the credit card companies involved in each round of his identity theft nightmare, but he has also considered applying for a new Social Insurance Number. While obtaining a new SIN is often a last resort, Guest may have to go to this extreme to protect himself from any future attacks. But changing your SIN isn't a foolproof method of protecting your good name either.

JOINING FORCES TO FIGHT IDENTITY THEFT AND FRAUD

The International Consumer Protection Enforcement Network (ICPEN) is a global organization that is "composed of consumer protection authorities from almost 40 countries." Their mandate is threefold: to "protect consumers' economic interests around the world, share information about cross-border commercial activities that may affect consumer welfare, [and to] encourage global cooperation among law enforcement agencies."

Canada is one of those 40 countries in the ICPEN. It's through our connection to this organization that law enforcement agencies across this nation, along with representatives from the Competition Bureau of Canada have, since 2009, continued to host Fraud Awareness Prevention Month every March.

Law enforcement agencies in Saskatchewan provide one example of how organizations work together to educate the public on the issues of identity theft and fraud. The Commercial Crime Section with RCMP "F" Division, the Regina Police Service, the

Saskatoon Police Service and the Saskatchewan Financial Services Commission join their resources to provide Saskatchewan residents with an educational blitz during Fraud Awareness Prevention Month. Every week throughout March, this law enforcement attack squad provides awareness campaigns about a wide variety of identity theft and fraud, often highlighting lesser-recognized scams in an effort to broaden their residents' overall knowledge. In 2011, one of the lesser-known topics the task force focused on was what is called the "reload scam."

Simply put, the reload scam targets previous victims of fraudulent investment opportunities. Typically, victims may not have noticed they had been taken advantage of or, if they had, the victims may not have yet had the chance to report the crime before being approached a second time. The alleged second party (in all honesty the original scammer could have re-presented him or herself) offers victims something they can't refuse—a chance to fix the mess and recoup their money. This second contact might even take the offer a step further and suggest they can do better than recover any money lost in the fraudulent transaction—they claim they can help the victim make a small profit and that they can do so quickly.

According to press information provided by the Saskatchewan RCMP, the reload scammer uses the victim's financial loss to entice him or her into selling the fraudulent stocks at a higher price than it originally cost the victim. There's a catch, however. The alleged buyer requires the victim to send a "purchase fee" first. You might wonder how, if the individual is aware they were scammed the first time around, they could believe the new offer is legitimate after having just lost money in a similar scam. But consider this.

The victim has already lost a considerable amount of money. In relation to the initial loss, the con artist making the new offer is probably asking for a much smaller amount of money. And if the offer works, a victim might argue, it might provide a way out of the bind, as well as a chance to turn a small profit.

Another profitable guise for the con artist and a more believable ruse for the victim is when contact is made between the two parties in the form of an official-sounding correspondence. In this approach, the con artist poses as an employee of a "government agency or foreign organization," offering to recover the victim's lost money. Again, a fee is required for the service, but because the offer looks official, vulnerable victims are tempted to fall for it.

The third version to this scam might be the most believable of all. In this rendition, the original victims of the fraudulent investment scheme are informed that the company holding the investments has gone bankrupt. But all it not lost! Another company with deeper pockets has devised a "plan to revive the original bankrupt company." Of course, a "fee per share cost" is charged to victims hoping the offer might be the answer to their loss. Unfortunately, as with the previous two renditions of this reload scam, any additional monies paid out end up in the same place as the victim's original investment—in the con artist's pocket.

What victims of this scam don't know is that following their initial contact with the scammer who talked them into the spurious investment opportunity in the first place, the victims' names have been circulated among a network of con artists. The thieves aren't averse to sharing information if it means they can reap financial rewards for themselves in the process.

It has been mentioned several times in this book and it's true again here: education is the key to protecting yourself from identity theft and identity fraud.

CHECKLIST FOR PROTECTING YOUR IDENTITY

Here are a few tips that at first glance seem to be common sense but are often overlooked given the right set of circumstances.

- Don't give anyone unguarded access to your personal information. Any private information you share must always be circumstance-specific. For example, your doctor doesn't need your Social Insurance Number. And under no circumstances should you provide the PIN to your debit or credit cards to anyone, not even a bank employee. Whenever you find yourself being questioned about personal details, ask yourself—or the person posing the question—if it is indeed necessary to the transaction that your personal information be given.

- Lock up *everything*—that includes your laptop, mailbox, house doors, vehicles, office doors, file cabinet drawers, desk drawers and cellphones. We all want to feel safe in our homes, workplaces and communities, but it's naïve to think we can trust everyone in our lives. And since we can't always predict which individual might be disingenuous, we have to be cautious with everyone.

- Monitor your mail for any fluctuations.

- Never give out personal information to someone who has contacted you by telephone or email.

- Cross-shred or burn every document that has any personal identification on it, even the address covers on your magazine subscriptions.

- We live in a society where we have passwords for everything—it can be a lot to remember. However, it's crucial you change these passwords at least twice a year, use a combination of upper and lower case letters and numbers, and create passwords that are at least eight characters long. Do not use passwords that are obvious, such as your telephone number or birth date. One source suggests that banks and credit card companies can refuse to cover any financial loss to individuals who have had their cards hacked because their PIN was weak.

- Do not carry unnecessary documents on your person. There is absolutely no need to have your SIN card, passport or birth certificate take up space in your wallet. Find a safe place to file these and other important items, such as in a safe-deposit box, and leave them there until you need them.

- Pay the nominal monthly fee required to keep your credit monitored. This not only provides you with a priceless peace of mind, it also ensures any changes to your credit are reported immediately via an email alert. For example, if you apply for a new credit card or mortgage, the company you employ will likely send you an email suggesting you visit your account online to verify you actually made that mortgage or credit card application. By purchasing this service, you can also review your credit profile and access the services of a credit specialist if necessary. If you are not inclined to purchase a monthly service, it is suggested that you check your credit report at least annually.

- Whenever you sell or give away a computer, cellphone or any other variety of personal digital assistant, make sure you've over-written the software. Note that it is difficult to permanently wipe your hard drive clean—knowledgeable hackers can often retrieve information that hasn't been properly erased. Be certain to thoroughly check your sources if you purchase a computer program online to do this for you—there is no end to the scam sites looking to make a quick buck off an uninformed customer. And if you're trading in your computer, ensure you are doing business with a reputable dealer you can trust and pay the necessary fee to have your hard drive professionally erased. Unfortunately, the safest method to deal with the personal information on a computer is to permanently destroy the equipment once you've finished with it.

ARE YOU A VICTIM?: VALUABLE STEPS IN RECOVERING YOUR GOOD NAME

Time is of the essence for anyone suspecting they've become a victim of identity theft: banks and credit card agencies cover most fraudulent transactions if you contact them within a short time of that occurrence. Below are a series of procedures suggested by organizations like the RCMP and the Canadian Anti-Fraud Centre should you believe you are a victim of identity theft:

- Contact one of the major credit reporting agencies and ask for a "fraud alert" to be placed on your name. Call Equifax at 1-800-465-7166, or TransUnion at 1-877-713-3393 for Québec residents, or 1-800-663-9980 for residents outside of Québec.

- Report your circumstances to the RCMP.

- Contact your banking and credit card institutions to report the theft or loss of any cards and provide them with date and time details surrounding that loss.

- Set aside a binder or notebook to record every contact you make during the entire process of reporting your situation and recovering your identity. This could take several months, or perhaps years, so organization is key if you are to successfully clear your name and maintain your good credit rating. Record the date and time of every contact you reach, or every contact made to you, along with the names or employee numbers of the individuals you conversed with and the details of every conversation surrounding your personal situation.

- Call the Canadian Anti-Fraud Centre at 1-888-495-8501 to obtain an Identity Theft Statement form (see Appendix). This form can also be downloaded directly from the website and filed electronically at www.antifraudcentre.ca. Filing an Identity Theft Statement provides victims with clear and detailed information about the crime in a professional format that they can then use to supply banking and credit card companies, utility companies and all other businesses, governments or associations requiring this information. It's also a good idea to register with the Canadian Anti-Fraud Centre as soon as you've discovered you've been victimized.

Chapter Three

Criminal Profile: Albert J. Walker

~

Although identity theft is often a precursor to fraudulent endeavours, absconding with someone else's identity after a crime has been committed affords a career criminal the chance to avoid detection by the authorities and to start life over again.

This is especially true if the person whose identity has been stolen is dead—and no one knows about it.

THE MAN BEHIND THE NAME

Albert Johnson Walker might have been a high school dropout, but it wasn't because of a lack of ability on his part. Perhaps boredom was the issue; perhaps he didn't find his lessons challenging enough. Or maybe he didn't like to listen to authority. Whatever the reason, Walker abandoned any chance at furthering his education by stepping out of the classroom and into the work world before what many would suggest was advisable.

For a few years after he left high school at the young age of 16, Walker seemed to flounder, taking whatever job he stumbled upon until he eventually enrolled with the University of Waterloo. It took Walker five years to earn two years' worth of courses as a mature student—it appeared extra-curricular socializing was more to Walker's liking than a serious investment in his studies. It was while socializing at one of the university's youth groups that Walker met Barbara McDonald, a serious, honest woman who was as dedicated to her studies as she was to her family and her faith. She was taken in by Walker's sometimes-exuberant personality, and the two were quickly an item and, after a relatively short courtship, married.

Walker and his new wife continued with their studies for a time, but Walker dropped out in favour of exploring the world of work. After several fits and starts he took a job at the Dana Porter Library at his old alma mater. Barbara, who successfully completed her studies, took a librarian position at a Kitchener-Waterloo library.

In 1978, a decade after Albert and Barbara tied the knot, they founded Walker Financial Services Incorporated, a "small payroll and income tax services company." Walker had been working as a life insurance agent with Mutual Life of Canada, and Barbara prepared income tax returns to moonlight her work at the library, so the new business venture represented a natural progression of their joint work experience. Two years after founding Walker Financial, the couple purchased Oxford Bookkeeping Systems, a small company based in Woodstock, Ontario. Walker was only 32 years old and his career was flourishing—his clients likely never knew the self-assured family man, church elder and self-made entrepreneur they trusted with their money hadn't even graduated high school.

Over the next decade, Walker's business continued to grow. In 1982, Walker and his wife incorporated United Canvest Corporation

(Cayman) Ltd., an "off-shore investment holding company in Grand Cayman Island." The new company provided clients with an opportunity to purchase preferred shares; it was a "safe investment with significant tax returns," Walker told them. It was later discovered that Walker had issued false certificates to the tune of $3.2 million worth of investments—money that Walker was later accused of stealing or losing in bad investments. Walker wasn't worried. In retrospect, many of his investors might shake their heads at how much they trusted the man, but at that time they would have probably argued that Walker knew how to "make everything sound so reasonable."

In 1986 Walker established Walker's Capital Corporation, a company that was eventually listed on the Alberta Stock Exchange. And by 1987, Walker's Financial Services Inc. employed more than 30 staff and boasted as many as nine offices in the southern Ontario communities of Woodstock, Paris, Ayr, Hagersville, Brantford, Cambridge, Strathroy, Guelph and London. The smooth talker and smart dresser that he was, Walker managed to convince clients, close friends and even family members to invest millions of dollars, which he then used to buy into high-risk investments.

One newspaper account reported that in 1989, friends of Walker "entrusted [the financier] with nearly $9 million from real estate deals." Walker was taking increasingly risky chances and had started enjoying the freedom only money can buy. He began travelling the world and spending lavishly, and whatever investment gambles he continued to take didn't appear to cause him to lose any sleep, despite the fact that he frequently lost a lot of money in the process.

His wife, however, was getting increasingly uncomfortable—and more than just Walker's business practices disturbed her. Barbara and Walker split in the summer of 1990 after Walker admitted to Barbara that he'd been having an "ongoing relationship with another woman." It was a devastating discovery for his wife, one that Walker flaunted in front of Barbara to such an extent that it's amazing she didn't crack under the pressure.

But Walker's affair wasn't the worst experience Barbara had during the two decades she spent at her husband's side.

In 2002, long after the couple divorced and Walker was facing the consequences of a lifetime of bad decisions, Barbara penned the book *Dancing Devil: My Twenty Years with Albert Walker*. In it Barbara detailed how terrified she was of the man she said abused her emotionally, psychologically and physically. He was "a monster," she wrote, explaining how he abused not only her but the couple's four children as well, and how on several occasions Walker threatened to have her killed.

The book took up where the court battle ending the two-decade-long marriage left off. During the couple's divorce proceedings, Barbara detailed Walker's violent behaviour in an affidavit she filed in an Ontario civil court. She explained how Walker threatened to "blow [her] away" and that she would "get nothing if [she did] not do what he [told her] to do." And if there was ever any doubt the man would follow through with his threats, they were quickly dismissed when he broke into what was once the couple's home and physically assaulted Barbara—these and so many other scenarios are described in detail in Barbara's book.

Despite the reality of the situation, Walker was awarded custody of his two eldest children, Jill and Sheena. Barbara retained custody of the two younger ones, Duncan and Heather. Regardless what many might think, this judgment was at least a partial victory for Barbara. The life Walker knew and loved was beginning to crumble.

It was time to take drastic action. At some point during the time Walker and Barbara were facing each other in court, it became increasingly evident to Walker that there was only one way he could continue to live in the manner with which he had become accustomed. He needed a fresh start in a fresh place.

Walker's singular alternative to further that goal was to take on a new identity.

ENDLESS OPPORTUNITY

In the world of finance, Walker had made a solid niche for himself. But as clients were beginning to question what was happening with their money, as threats of bankruptcy loomed and as risky ventures turned sour, Walker planned his big escape. Court documents from 1998 state that while preparing for his escape, "a minimum $1,066,940.00 was withdrawn or transferred by Walker from the CIBC and Credit Suisse [an account he'd set up in Geneva, Switzerland] accounts he opened in his name in Toronto in 1990." Another million dollars was unaccounted for at the time of Walker's eventual disappearance, and it was later discovered Walker had also purchased $600,000 in gold bars. It was reasonable to conclude that wherever he went, Walker wasn't going to want for much.

The night before he boarded a plane to the UK, Walker dined with his children at a fancy restaurant. He told them he was setting off for a two-week-long trip to do business in England and Switzerland. That announcement wasn't too surprising.

However, his decision to take his 15-year-old daughter, Sheena, with him was somewhat startling.

Before boarding his plane to England on December 5, 1990, Walker stole one more thing. Unknown to anyone but himself, and perhaps Sheena, Walker assumed the name and identity of a former Walker Financial client who, many would later speculate, bore a remarkable resemblance to Walker. After stealing this former client's birth certificate, Walker left his old life behind in Canada and assumed his new identity as David Wallis Davis. He had his money, the potential for a new start and a "young bride" by his side: posing as his wife was none other than Sheena.

It's not clear what Walker was planning for the type of life he and his daughter would share when the two left Canada. Perhaps passing Sheena off as his wife was merely a curveball to throw off the authorities, who would probably be looking for a man and his daughter. And while the details of Walker's relationship with Sheena have been alluded to but never made public, and the young girl initially left with her father without any regret at the time, the tyranny under which she must have lived was no doubt considerable. When Walker eventually faced trial in 1998, Sheena was 22 years old. She was one of 36 witnesses to testify against the man. But during that plane trip before Christmas of 1990, and for the eight intervening years, no one who knew the two would have ever guessed the terrible secrets they harboured.

It was only going to get worse.

Back in Canada, Barbara was planning her Christmas cele-
brations and hoping Sheena would be part of the festivities. But
when Walker contacted his staff saying he wasn't going to make it to
the Christmas party they'd planned for that night—his flight was
allegedly detained in England because of a storm—she must have
felt a little more nervous than usual. When Christmas came and
went, and Barbara had yet to be reunited with her daughter and no
one had heard from Sheena, alarm bells were ringing loud and clear.

Walker's unexplained absence raised alarm bells with more
than the man's estranged wife. Investors were starting to question
why he hadn't returned home. On January 10, one of those suspicious
investors filed the first of several complaints that would trickle in to
the RCMP. John Moran of John Moran and Associates said he was
concerned about several discrepancies he'd discovered in Walker's
business dealings. For one thing, Walker had made several large
charges: $11,556 for a ring and other jewellery from a Birks store in
Toronto and "$12,542 in first-class British Airways tickets from Ele-
gant Tours of Toronto." As well, Moran had handed Walker almost
$46,000 to purchase shares with one of Walker's companies.

With every passing day, officials were discovering more discrepancies, and within a couple of months of Walker's disappearance, it was evident that Walker was anything but the honest and
trustworthy investor he presented himself to be.

Across the Atlantic, Walker's deceit was escalating to an
entirely new level.

A NEW LIFE, A NEW SET OF RULES

Once settled in Britain, Walker continued to live under his assumed alias. He also continued to con his way into people's lives to further his own means—a talent he was becoming well known for back in Canada.

Walker recognized that passing himself off as David Wallis Davis had to be an interim strategy. He couldn't risk being connected to his former client—that kind of connection would land the authorities on his doorstep in no time.

Walker knew he needed to acquire a more permanent identity, one that supplied him with all the essential paperwork necessary should anyone ever question him down the road. And so his first order of business was to find a gullible target that would match his own general age and physical description and provide Walker with yet another new identity.

Enter Elaine Boyes. The art store clerk working in the city of Harrogate was perhaps one of the most unfortunate individuals to meet the con man going by the name of Davis. Walker first met Boyes at the art store, engaged her in lengthy conversation and finished off by offering her a job "to buy and sell antiques." All she had to do was travel to Europe and exchange "currency into British pounds."

Boyes would later tell the authorities she was initially taken with Walker's easy manner, but when he lingered for two hours and didn't give any indication he was planning to leave, she became uncomfortable. When she agreed to consider his offer, Walker left the store. He told her he'd call her in a couple of weeks. During their conversation, Walker had learned Elaine and her boyfriend had a dream of going to Canada. Walker suspected the couple offered him the perfect opportunity for a new identity. And so two weeks after his first visit with Elaine, he called her again and suggested he meet with her and her beau and discuss his business offer over a cup of tea.

It was through that second meeting with Boyes that Walker met Ronald J. Platt—another man who looked a lot like Walker. Boyes and the quiet, hard-working television repairman had been an item for quite some time, and Walker was convinced the pair would want to share the new adventure in business with him. Better still, Platt couldn't wait to get to know the suave Walker and his young wife better.

According to court documents, a short while into the new friendship, Walker had managed to convince Boyes and Platt to:

…incorporate a company in England for his sole benefit, operation and control called Cavendish Corporation Limited. Platt and Boyes were registered as the company's directors and officers, and Elaine Boyles as the sole shareholder of the company signed an agreement whereby she agreed to hold her shares as nominee for Walker. After Cavendish Corporation Limited was incorporated Walker alone controlled it, and Elaine Boyes and Ronald J. Platt carried out tasks as instructed by Walker including, among other things, opening bank accounts in England and in the company's name and operating them as instructed. Elaine Boyes and Ronald J. Platt were also persuaded by Walker to open bank accounts in their personal names in England, Switzerland, France, and Italy and to do

banking in respect of these accounts as instructed by Walker
ostensibly as part of his carrying on the business of Cavendish
Corporation Limited....

Phase one complete, Walker moved on to the next step in his master plan. Walker knew the 47-year-old Platt was originally from Britain but as a young lad had immigrated with his father to Calgary. Even though Platt's family eventually returned to Britain, Platt always hoped to return—if there was ever any doubt about his affection for Canada, all anyone had to do was look at the maple leaf tattooed on his hand. So in 1992, as a Christmas gift to his dear friends, Walker handed Boyes and Platt two one-way plane tickets to Calgary. The couple left in February 1993, but not before Platt gave Walker his driver's licence and birth certificate, chequebooks and credit cards: Walker explained that these documents were necessary for Walker to be able to settle any debts Platt and Boyes might have in Britain. Walker also obtained "rubber stamps made of [the couple's] signatures. Further, Elaine Boyes executed a general power of attorney in favour of Walker." In exchange for their extensive cooperation, Walker provided the couple with seed money to start out their new life in Canada.

Having landed the perfect candidates for his scheme, Walker had most assuredly addressed every potential eventuality. Unbelievably, Walker had managed to procure everything he needed to remake himself yet again. And it appeared that the real Ronald Platt was quite happy to help his friend in any way he could, even if he was somewhat unaware of the type of help he was supplying. Not only had Walker managed to establish a means with which to incur a steady income, but with Platt's help he also managed to acquire another identity. As soon as Platt and Boyes boarded the plane to Canada, Walker assumed Ronald Platt's identity. His "wife" Sheena would now go by the name Noelle. If Walker had any concerns that the authorities back home had connected the dots and discovered that he had been using Davis' ID, this new cover should throw them off the trail a good while longer.

Business transactions conducted through Cavendish Corporation Limited no doubt resulted in some form of financial windfall for Walker, but details about that have not been made public. Still, the business foundation Walker laid with Platt and Boyes gave the Canadian added reassurance that he'd be able to continue living his new life and perhaps expand his personal worth. Walker had retained much of the considerable stash he'd left Canada with in 1990, and he and Sheena had been living quite comfortably on that money, but it wouldn't last forever.

Springing for the two plane tickets to Calgary got Platt out of the picture, removing any possible confusion among Platt's friends and acquaintances. The deception provided Walker with access to bank accounts and credit lines he otherwise wouldn't have had. For the next couple of years, the real Platt and his British girlfriend strived to establish a new start for themselves in Canada. At the same time, Walker and his daughter, along with the addition of two baby girls, Emily and Lily, whose parentage has never been publicly acknowledged, lived a relatively "peaceful" existence, having set up house in London, Harrogate and Devon before finally settling in at the hamlet of Woodham Walter, a village north of Brentwood Essex. Even if someone might have questioned the age difference between the man and his "wife," or the fact that Emily, Lily and "their mother" Sheena all called Walker "Daddy," or uncovered any other discrepancy that may have raised an eyebrow or two, Walker's gentle-looking face, his calm outward demeanour and his professional persona gave him a sense of credibility that worked in his favour.

Life would have quite likely continued along without disruption if it hadn't been for an unfortunate change of luck for the real Platt and Boyes. By 1994, Ron Platt was pawning anything he could to raise money after falling on tough times. He and Boyes had parted ways; devastated by the breakup and homesick for England, Elaine Boyes returned to the UK.

Hoping to hang on to his dream, Ron scrimped through life in Calgary for a bit longer before he too headed back to England in 1995. Maybe Walker, aka Davis, aka Platt—unbeknownst to the real Platt—might help him get back on his feet.

Ron could only hope.

When Ron reappeared on the scene in 1995, Walker and Sheena were living in Woodham Walter. At that point Walker was passing himself off as a psychotherapist and worked with three other Essex-based psychotherapists offering self-improvement workshops across Britain.

At the same time, Walker was always on the lookout for ways to make extra cash, anxious to continue living in the manner with which he had become accustomed. Ever the con man and adept at targeting just the right kind of trusting person, Walker put on his financial advisor hat and set his sights on 81-year-old Frank Johnson. The pensioner and his girlfriend, Audrey Mossman, lived next door to the Platts. Walker told the trusting Johnson that he was once an executive with Citibank and that he had a great investment opportunity for the octogenarian, promising him a big return on his investment. Johnson gave Walker about $400,000—Johnson never saw most of that money again.

Despite any setbacks Walker might have experienced, he wasn't worried that his real identity would ever be discovered even though Canadian authorities were looking for him. Whenever a situation arose to cause any concern, it was never so troublesome that a simple move to another community wouldn't fix it.

At least he wasn't remotely stressed until he heard a knock on his door one day and opened it to find the man whose identity he'd stolen standing on the front stoop of his two-storey farmhouse.

You Can Never Go Home

The real Ronald Platt had tried everything he could to hang on to his Canadian dream but in the end he had to admit that he had run out of options. He loved the country, but with no family, limited friends and no real employment prospects, Ronald felt his only alternative was to return to England and reconnect with his one true friend.

Platt explained to Walker that he'd moved back to England and was living close by. The two old friends could pick up where they left off, Platt must have suggested. After all, the two men were still business partners, were they not?

Ronald's arrival must have provided Walker with one of the few significant shocks in the con man's life. He was pretty good at dancing with danger. He was convincing in his assumed identity and had managed to keep Sheena in line all this time. But Walker would have been hard-pressed to keep up the ruse that he was Ronald Platt with the real Ronald Platt living so close.

There was only one answer to his problem—and the solution plunged Walker into an entirely new category of identity thief.

While the authorities in Canada knew the con man as Albert Johnson Walker, and the Brits that Walker had befriended and worked with called him Platt, Ronald still referred to his Canadian friend as Davis. Perhaps Platt was hoping for some form of financial compensation from the company he and his former girlfriend had helped Walker establish or, at the very minimum, a helping hand to get back on his feet again. Walker no doubt recognized that he had to do something for Platt or the entire sham Walker was living would explode in no time.

To smooth the situation over until he came up with a more permanent solution, Walker helped Ronald settle into an apartment in Chelmsford, Essex, and gave the landlord the name Davis David as Ronald's reference. For several months Walker maintained contact with his namesake, although to Ronald it was obvious the relationship between the two men had changed significantly since the Brit had left for Canada. As talented a fraudster as he was, Walker must have struggled with living out two personas at one time, and his temperament showed his irritation with this sudden kink in his plans.

But Walker was pretty adept at picking himself up and refocusing his efforts whenever he had come up against roadblocks. This time was no different. Plan A might have failed, but Walker had no problem coming up with Plan B.

In July 1996, Walker and his family took a holiday in Devon, where Walker still kept a 24-foot Trident sailboat called the *Lady Jane*. Sheena spent most of the holiday with her father, but one day he announced he was going sailing alone. He was gone the entire day, but Sheena didn't mind being left behind. It was July 20, the first day of the Atlanta Olympics, and Sheena was excited about the chance to catch the television coverage of the opening ceremonies.

Walker invited Platt along for a day of sailing, but he didn't tell Sheena about it. There was good reason for Walker's deception, and he had no intention of anyone ever uncovering what was about to become one of his most grisly secrets.

Eight days later, while Walker and his family were at home and back to their daily routine, the salty sea air now only a memory, commercial fisherman Jim Copik was in his boat, the *Malkerry*, trawling the English Channel. Pulling in his nets, the fisherman noticed his haul felt considerably heavier than usual. What Copik managed to pull on to his boat was far from an ordinary catch.

There, tangled in his net amid the best catch of his day, was the body of a middle-aged man, along with a 10-pound, galvanized steel anchor. The fisherman didn't find a wallet or any other personal items that might identify the man. And although he contacted the authorities, Copik made one error in judgment—he gave away the anchor. He didn't need another anchor, but he knew someone who did. Thinking he was doing a good deed, Copik passed it on.

The absence of identification left the police stumped for a time. Initially, the authorities questioned whether the unfortunate gentleman might have been depressed and committed suicide.

Or perhaps the dead man was a sailor and had accidentally fallen overboard?

An autopsy confirmed that the cause of death was indeed drowning, but the coroner discovered additional injuries on the corpse. Namely, the deceased had suffered from a head injury prior to his drowning, and it looked like the anchor, which was finally recovered, might have been the cause of that injury. Additional forensic testing suggested that the anchor had been secured to the man's belt, leaving investigators with the horrific conclusion that the man had been knocked unconscious, weighted down and then thrown into the English Channel to die a cold and watery death.

It was now confirmed: the police had a murder on their hands. But before they could examine the series of events that led to the man's demise, the authorities had the daunting task of having to identify the man first.

One item that had not been removed from the man before tossing him into the sea was a Rolex watch. The watch was the valuable piece of evidence that offered the clues necessary to put a name to the victim, who was dubbed "The Rolex Man." Because Rolex wristwatches have serial numbers and are engraved each time they are serviced, British police were able to identify the man sporting the pricy timepiece as none other than Ronald Joseph Platt.

The Rolex's calendar offered up another essential piece to the puzzle, namely a solid estimate as to when the man was murdered. By noting the date on the watch and factoring in that a Rolex is waterproof and will continue to run for two to three days when inactive, police could estimate when Platt was murdered.

After tracing the deceased man to his last known address in Chelmsford, police contacted Platt's reference: David Davis. The telephone call must have been the second most significant shock of Walker's life, but the fraudster maintained his composure and carefully answered the officer's questions. Strange as the entire case seemed to the police, they still hadn't uncovered anything that could lead them to a motive for murder, or a possible murderer.

After making every effort to trace Platt's movements and coming up empty-handed, the mystery of The Rolex Man was about to be closed when fate intervened. On his way to inform Davis that chances were the man's friend's death would remain unsolved, Essex police Detective Sergeant Peter Redman took a wrong turn.

Instead of pulling up to the Little London Farmhouse where Walker and his family lived, they pulled into the Little London House belonging to Walker's neighbour, Frank Johnson. When Redman told Johnson he was looking for the man's neighbour, David Davis, Redman was surprised to learn that no one by that name lived next door. Instead, Johnson told Redman that the name of his neighbour was none other than Ronald Platt.

Needless to say, the pronouncement put an entirely new spin on the investigation. Who was this man, David Davis? And why was he masquerading as Ronald Platt? When Redman pulled out of Johnson's driveway, he made a beeline back to the station to see what he could uncover.

The plot, as they say, would thicken before the authorities were able to make any sense out of the case of The Rolex Man and the mysterious Mr. Davis.

IDENTIFYING THE SUSPECT

Walker was arrested on charges of murdering Ronald Platt the morning of October 31, 1996. After he was fingerprinted, it became evident that David Davis was actually Albert Johnson Walker, Canada's most wanted fugitive at the time and number four on Interpol's Most Wanted list. Prior to his discovery under an assumed name, Walker was wanted for theft and fraud charges totalling an estimated $3.2 million.

Now he was also a person of interest in a murder investigation and identity theft.

Finding Walker living under Platt's name, and the new evidence that Walker was hiding from the authorities in Canada, cleared up a few unexplained questions. In particular, it gave investigators a motive for why Walker might want to murder Platt. Now they faced the difficult task of having to prove it.

The first step in their investigation was to interview Walker's "wife," Noelle. Of course, nothing in the investigation to that point was what it seemed, and it was rapidly becoming evident that Walker's "wife" wasn't anything they expected. She was a lot younger than Walker for one—young enough to be his daughter. In fact, she bore a striking resemblance to his daughter Sheena. The police had photographs of the pair after having contacted the Canadian authorities and discovering that Walker and Sheena had been missing since 1990. Could it be that Walker was masquerading his own offspring as his wife? The possibility was unthinkable. And yet, when presented with the suggestion, Sheena confessed that she indeed was the fraudster's daughter.

During the course of the investigation, Sheena provided considerable information about Walker's whereabouts in the days leading up to and following Platt's death. She explained that the family had holidayed in Devon and stayed at a hotel in Totnes. She said she'd spent every day with her father except one—the day he wanted to go out on his boat alone. Sheena couldn't put a date to that day, but when she explained she'd been watching the opening ceremonies of the Atlanta Olympics, investigators were able to pinpoint the date as the same day they believed Platt had been murdered. When police contacted the hotel's management, they learned that the Walkers had stayed there under the name Davis. Hotel management also explained that Walker met with another individual named Ronald Platt. The physical description they gave of Walker's male companion matched that of the deceased man, right down to the maple leaf tattoo on the back of his hand.

From there, police combed through Platt's sailboat. A detailed forensic investigation confirmed that Platt's fingerprints were found on a discarded plastic bag. It was from a retail outlet called "Sport Nautique," the same store Walker had purchased a 10-pound galvanized steel anchor a few days before his vacation. In addition, "three head hairs attached to a piece of cellular material had been discovered on a cushion inside the cabin of the yacht." DNA analysis confirmed the hairs belonged to Ronald Platt and that they "had been removed from the head…as a result of some form of trauma, such as a blow to the head, rather than the normal process of hair being naturally shed." Another damning piece of evidence was the sailboat's GPS, which placed the boat at the exact location about 9.5 kilometres out to sea off south Devon at 8:59 on the evening of July 20, 1996.

Walker's murder trial opened on June 22, 1998, in Exeter Crown Court. Although Walker pleaded not guilty to the murder of Ronald Platt during his preliminary hearing on April 27, 1998, he was found guilty and faced a life sentence in a British prison without eligibility for parole for 15 years.

Of course, that wasn't the end of Walker's story. Canadian authorities still had an international arrest warrant out on the man. But would Walker ever face the more than 20 charges of fraud on the other side of the Atlantic? And what ever happened to the roughly $3 million Walker allegedly made away with?

According to Ontario Supreme Court documents dated April 27, 1998, police in England had seized Walker's assets following his arrest. These assets included:

(a) *One sail boat purchased for £4500 by Walker for his own benefit using the name Ronald J. Platt;*

(b) *Two oil paintings purchased for £5275 by Walker for his own benefit using the name David Davis;*

(c) *Three oil paintings purchased for £14,415 by Walker in the name of Cavendish Corporation Limited;*

(d) *Ten 500 gram gold bars purchased for £47,330 by Walker for his own benefit using the name Ronald J. Platt;*

(e) *Five 10 ounce gold bars purchased for $22,620 by Walker for his own benefit under his name in Toronto before fleeing Canada;*

(f) *Two 1 kilo gold bars purchased for £19,994 by Walker for his own benefit using the name Ronald J. Platt.*

Furthermore, "…as part of the arrest of Walker the English police authorities also seized and are in possession of £25,600 and 8179 Swiss francs. With the exception of £4020 in the possession of Sheena Davis upon her arrest the balance of the funds were discovered in various premises rented by Walker. The funds Walker had access to and used during his stay in England to live on and to purchase all assets had their origin in funds misappropriated by him from Ontario…"

In addition to these assets, the court documents revealed almost two dozen different bank accounts scattered in various Canadian banks, along with accounts in Switzerland, England, France, Cayman Island and Italy.

While investigators were procuring what essentially amounted to a treasure hunt in an effort to unveil the millions Walker swindled from friends, family members and trusting elderly clients, they only managed to recover the equivalent of $1 million in assets. But it was enough. It was looking as though the man who'd evaded custody for so long was going to need to recreate himself once again, this time in a British prison.

But in April 1998, once the verdict was in and Walker was found guilty of murder, authorities on both sides of the pond expected Walker would live out his life sentence in Britain. While it was small comfort to his Canadian victims, everyone breathed a collective sigh of relief that the man had finally received some form of punishment for his crimes.

Once again, Walker's story was not over.

By February 2005, after serving seven years of his sentence, Correctional Service of Canada announced Walker was being transferred to a Canadian jail. It wasn't the first time Walker had applied for a transfer; in 2001 his Toronto lawyer Scott Fenton prepared a similar request under the Transfer of Offenders Act and Treaty. That first bid was turned down, but it was approved in 2005 because of what the authorities called "humanitarian" reasons. "Transfers of this nature are normally humanitarian in nature," Holly Knowles, Corrections Canada spokeswoman told Canadian Press reporters. "Often it's better in terms of community support, family contacts, reintegration potential, [and] access to health care."

Now 59, Walker was reportedly sick and wanted to be closer to his family. In exchange for the consideration, he'd reportedly agreed to "reveal the location of the money he stole" in the hope of reducing his time behind bars, although sources have yet to confirm whether he followed through with that promise.

The announcement of Walker's transfer surprised his family. "There's no need for him to come back," Walker's ex-wife Barbara McDonald told Colleen Toms of *The Expositor*. "If he's ill, don't they have doctors and medical care in England? He doesn't need to come back here."

Walker's fraud victims shared McDonald's sentiments.

"He's supposed to rot in jail," John Slaman told Canadian Press reporters in another news story. "Do we need a guy like that back in Canada?… A lot of people, as well as his (former) wife and his kids, are suffering once again because of his return. That doesn't do any good to anybody to have the guy come back."

"His family doesn't want any part of him," Walker's former brother-in-law, Ken "Jiggs" McDonald told *Toronto Sun* reporters Tom Godfrey and Alan Cairns. "They are living in fear of him... This man is a con man who is capable of anything—I wouldn't put anything past him."

Despite the public outrage, Walker arrived back in Canada on February 24, 2005. In 2007, Walker pleaded guilty to 20 charges of fraud in this country. He was sentenced to four years in jail for the fraud and another year for the charge of violating the Bankruptcy Act. The five years were to be served concurrent to his former sentence.

The victims of Walker's fraudulent dealings had to wait considerably longer to get the justice they wanted. And when KPMG, the company appointed to collect and sell off any of Walker's remaining assets and unravel the financier's spiderweb of dealings, announced they had finally finished handling the estate, Walker's victims were no doubt less than satisfied. According to a QMI Agency report dated June 27, 2011, once the costs incurred by KPMG and associated parties were settled to the tune of $481,038, the "trustee distributed a total of $608,392 to five preferred and 73 unsecured creditors."

Walker was eligible to apply for day parole in 2010, but at last report he had not exercised his right to do so. He is eligible to apply for full parole on March 12, 2013. Whenever he does get out, Walker might not find any family members interested in connecting with him and find his friends about as faithful to him as he'd been to his friend Ronald Platt.

As one of Walker's past clients so eloquently put it to *Sun* reporters Jane Sims and Patrick Maloney, "I don't hate anybody, but I want him to stay in jail…he had charisma and he could still have it. If he's in jail, everybody's protected."

The criminal profile of Albert Walker proves that although identity theft can be used to line someone's pocketbook, even murder isn't ruled out when the threat of capture and a prison sentence looms large.

Chapter Four

Scamming the Information Highway

~

INTERNET FRAUD

We live in an era when, if we own a computer and are plugged into the Internet, almost anything the world has to offer is but a keystroke away. For example, if you use Google, you can search whatever is on your mind at any given moment and within 0.19 seconds or less, you'll find thousands or even millions of options to click on that provide you with the information as well as countless bits of intelligence, advice or trivial facts you have absolutely no interest in.

Clearly, the computer age is a wonder to behold. The variety of opportunities it offers for personal and professional advancement are endless. But this vast array of possibilities also opens the door for opportunists who will stop at nothing to exploit these prospects for their own gain. It's as if another tool was presented among the assorted weaponry in a criminal's arsenal. And while most of us were celebrating the advent of a new technology, nefarious marauders were looking for ways to mine that information in order to illegally line their pocketbooks.

It wouldn't be long before society's most personal, private and confidential information was available to anyone tech-savvy enough to break through the firewalls designed to protect us against such an invasion.

A New Age Dawns

Many Canadians probably remember first hearing talk about an "information highway" back in the early 1990s. This electronic means of communicating between computers was first examined as far back as 1967 and had its beginnings with the U.S. military. The Defense Advanced Research Projects Agency (DARPA) is the arm of the U.S. Department of Defense whose mission it is to "maintain the technological superiority of the U.S. military and prevent technological surprise from harming our national security by sponsoring revolutionary, high-payoff research bridging the gap between fundamental discoveries and their military use."

DARPA, which back in the 1960s went by the name Advanced Research Projects Agency (ARPA), began work on the creation of an information highway by building on the idea of linking "time-sharing computers into a national system." The agency contracted the Stanford Research Institute in Menlo Park, California, to design a workable prototype for this electronic means of transporting information. And in 1969 the first nodes were installed at the Stanford Research Institute and the University of California, Los Angeles (UCLA).

To test their efforts, UCLA engineering professor Leonard Kleinrock and student Charley Kline typed in the word "login" and proceeded to send the one-word message from their computer to a computer located at another one of Stanford's research and technology centres in Palo Alto, California, more than 600 kilometres away. That first message was partially successful—only the letters "lo" made their way across that first bumpy road, and it took considerable time for the two letters to reach their destination—but the foundation had been set for the most intricate highway project in history.

It wasn't until 1971 that "the world's first network email system" was established on what was originally known as the Advanced Research Projects Agency Network (ARPANET). From that point it was like the Garden of Eden all over again—there was no turning back. The apple had been consumed; the Internet was making its way into most homes across North America, providing residents with the ability to communicate from one computer to another across one nation and around the world.

By 1985 every Canadian university was connected by the analogous system known as NetNorth. By 1989 more than 100,000 Internet hosts had been established across the globe, birthing the term "World Wide Web" and the Internet address precursor www. And despite the fact that by 1993 more than 15 million people were tuned in, and as CBC's Bill Cameron said, "The Internet is growing like an embryonic brain at a rate of 10 percent a month," a large segment of society was suspicious of the new technology and remained stubbornly unconvinced it would become a household item like televisions and radios had a generation earlier.

Of course the disbelievers were wrong. In 2009, it was estimated that 77.7 percent of Canadians use the Internet, which represents 26 million users, and that number continues to rise, albeit less ferociously than it had during the Internet's infancy.

With access to 77.7 percent of the residents of this country, potentially representing 26 million pocketbooks, with similar percentages in the United States and other developed countries (InternetWorldStats.com suggests there are about 1.17 billion users worldwide), the unscrupulous people living among us see nothing but dollar signs. If a crook can con as little as one dollar from every individual represented in these figures, he or she can become a millionaire overnight.

Quite aware of this unique opportunity to turn one buck into thousands, the criminal element has found numerous opportunities to mine the information highway even as the foundations for this new technology were still being developed. While computer and software specialists were developing programs to make life easier for the private and public sector alike, scammers and fraudsters were tapping into those vessels of information with only one thought in mind—to find a crack in security that would allow them to dig into personal and secret information. Once they retrieved that information, huge profits could be harvested at the expense of unaware victims.

In an effort to remotely control a computer and mine its secrets, a computer virus temporarily disabled ARPANET as early as 1980. Researchers had written a handful of experimental programs in the latter part of the 1970s. Computer hackers weren't far behind in honing into this new technology, and phishing for dollars has become their new favourite sport.

YOU'VE GOT MAIL

Christmas is expensive, no matter how frugal a shopper might be. But the holiday season of 2005 was unexpectedly expensive for BC resident Val Broeckx. Most times she has a pretty good idea about what she has charged to her credit card, but when she opened her MasterCard bill that December, she was stunned to see her balance was considerably larger than she had expected.

Reading through the list of charges and comparing them to the receipts she kept for cross-reference, Val realized that a $1000 charge attributed to PayPal was not backed up with a receipt. She was absolutely certain she had made no such charge to her credit card. Val didn't routinely use PayPal, a company that offers an easy and relatively safe method to pay for goods electronically by encrypting sensitive financial information.

"I was freaked," Val told reporters with CBC *Marketplace*. "I knew something majorly wrong had happened. I knew I hadn't used my PayPal in over a year."

Searching her mind for clues about the bogus charge, Val recalled an email she had received from PayPal not long before the charge was made. The email had requested her to update her personal information for their files. Since the email looked legitimate, she had complied with the request. That was her big mistake. Once Val filled in the information, the fraudster initially targeting her computer was provided with her personal data.

This brand of email fraud is an Internet scam known as phishing. As defined by the Canadian Anti-Fraud Centre, phishing is "a general term for email, text messages and websites fabricated and sent by criminals and designed to look like they come from well-known and trusted businesses, financial institutions and government agencies in an attempt to collect personal, financial and sensitive information."

Also known as brand spoofing, phishing email schemes look legitimate, with recognizable company fonts, letterheads and contact information that in many cases are verifiable if you were to view the company's website directly. This is the most dangerous email scam because it can trip up the most scrupulous reader. However, this kind of email request is *never* legitimate. Email communications from legitimate companies were once the norm, but best practices dictate they are not the chosen method of business for companies today. Businesses that still rely on email communication with their customers, mobile telephone companies for example, might initially contact their clients by email, but they will usually tell customers to respond to the message by logging on to their account through that company's Internet home page.

Here is an example of a recent phishing attempt that used PayPal as its front:

Information Regarding Your account:

Dear PayPal Member:

Attention! Your PayPal account has been limited!

As part of our security measures, we regularly screen activity in the PayPal system. We recently contacted you after noticing an issue on your account. *We requested information from you for the following reason:*

Our system detected unusual charges to a credit card linked to your PayPal account.

Reference Number: PP-259-187-991

This is the Last reminder to log in to PayPal as soon as possible. Once you log in, you will be provided with steps to restore your account access.

Once you log in, you will be provided with steps to restore your account access. We appreciate your understanding as we work to ensure account safety.

[At this point the email requests the reader to "click here" to activate their account and access what the writer claims to be a "safe" site. The email then closes with the following pleasantries.]

We thank you for your prompt attention to this matter. Please understand that this is a security measure intended to help protect you and your account. We apologise for any inconvenience.

Sincerely,

PayPal Account Review Department

All rights reserved.

PayPal Ltd.

PayPal FSA Register Number: 226056.

PayPal Email ID PP059

[This spammer then adds another layer of convincing propaganda, allegedly providing some helpful hints to safeguard the reader's online safety. Of course, this is simply one more way of looking legitimate and calming any apprehensions the email recipient may have about responding to the request.]

Protect Your Account Info

Make sure you never provide your password to fraudulent websites.

To safely and securely access the PayPal website or your account, open a new web browser (e.g. Internet Explorer or Netscape) and type in the PayPal login page [an authentic-looking Internet address was included here] *to be sure you are on the real PayPal site.*

For more information on protecting yourself from fraud, please review our Security Tips at [another address link was posted here, which included the name "PayPal"].

PROTECT YOUR PASSWORD

Never Give Your PayPal Password to Anyone

Authentic-looking emails like the example given can send our blood pressure soaring. The writer has used sound psychology in addressing his readers by using the following criteria.

- The approach is clear and direct.

- He begins by stating that PayPal has initiated action to protect the recipient from questionable activity on their account.

- The email highlights the "unusual charges" it questions on the credit card linked to the reader's account.

- A lengthy reference number is thrown in—something that appears complicated tends to lend itself to a sense of legitimacy in our unconscious mind.

- The reader is asked to log in to his or her account to reactivate it.

- The reader is prompted for a quick response, and a profuse apology is given for any inconvenience experienced as a result of the email.

- Official-looking company copyright dates and registration information is listed.

- And as if this wasn't enough, the email ends with ways to safeguard personal information.

With all the official-looking mastheads and logos in the email, it's easy to understand how someone might be fooled.

Scammers using banking institutions as a cover for their frauds have used similar approaches when attempting to elicit personal information from email recipients. It seems like common sense to ignore these attempts at prying open your pocketbook, but when an email arrives from the bank you use or a company you patronize, such as PayPal, the most levelheaded among us might be tempted to check it out. It's natural for human beings to react out of fear or emotion instead of stepping back and thinking objectively for a few moments. But it's crucial to think before you act—take a physical and mental step back and think through the email with a cautious mindset:

- Do not click on any links in the email.

- Do not dial the telephone number or use the website information included in the email—go directly to the Internet and Google the company name from there.

- Telephone or visit your banking representative in person to inquire about your account.

- Directly contact any other place of business sending an email with similar claims.

The more the public learns about the dangers of spam mail and how important it is not to click on the links provided in those messages, the more tricks the writers of these emails contrive. In my own case, when I copied the contents of one fake PayPal email and pasted it into a Word document in writing this chapter, I inadvertently clicked on the masthead. That misstep immediately opened a window on my Internet browser that flashed a warning message stating I'd logged on to a suspected phishing site. I did not click a link, and yet I'd done enough to put me, and my computer, in potential danger—it certainly wasn't something I intended to do. My intent is not to advocate paranoia but to point out that it's crucial to use meticulous discretion, without exception, when dealing with online communications.

And if you are targeted, like Val Broeckx was, don't back down. When Broeckx noticed the bogus $1000 charge on her credit card, she didn't sit back and let it slide. She contacted her credit card company and PayPal immediately, explaining she had not made the charge listed. She also traced the company associated with the charge, looking for an explanation. In the process, Val's story exposed another online scheme that many innocent individuals have fallen victim to.

GET RICH QUICK…I PROMISE

Work-at-home schemes have been around for a long time, but the ease of email access means they now reach a larger audience. Simply put, the more people who read the ads that offer allegedly lucrative opportunities, the more likely the ads are to fall into the hands of someone suffering a job loss, tough financial circumstances, business struggles or physical limitations that make holding down a traditional job difficult. When presented with an opportunity to work smarter, not harder, and turn a profit in the process, especially when it lands directly on your home computer, it can seem like an answer to prayer.

As Val Broeckx and Derek Hannah will tell you, these offers only answer the greedy prayers of anonymous crooks—they are nothing more than another kind of cover for another unscrupulous phishing expedition.

According to the 2005 CBC *Marketplace* story, the $1000 charge on Broeckx's credit card was connected to a company named Rugged Cross Recordings. Broeckx traced the company to Derek Hannah, a struggling Christian rocker from New Jersey. The trusting family man answered an online ad to work from home. His job was to "transfer money to an offshore company" in the Ukraine.

Although some might suggest it is obvious that the following email is corrupt, it's one of many such offers that intrigue some readers to open the email, if only for curiosity's sake. And if you do open the email, you may end up opening your computer to clever hackers on the other end instead of finding a link to your own personal pot of gold. Or you'll connect yourself with someone who isn't interested in your welfare and might use you to further his or her own criminal activities.

From: MJD007@SHSU.EDU

Subject: Thank You Dear

Date: January 29, 2012 5:48:15 PM GMT-06:00

Reply-To: [XXXXXX]@mail.com

Greetings,

I have a 100% risk free partnership business proposition worth 6.5 million dollars for you. Contact me with my private email address [XXXXXX] for details. I promise you won't regret it as it will benefit us greatly.

Regards,

Carolina

Other email "business propositions" seem legitimate because they appear to be quite straightforward about their underhanded dealings. The following example makes no bones about the fact that the writer is on a desperate hunt for someone to "secretly" launder money. The recipient of the email might not be opposed to a little deceit every now and again, especially if the opportunity being offered smoothes out their financial struggles.

The next email uses sound psychology—among the huge number of individuals who receive the email, a handful might reply. The offer isn't a sure path to easy street—it's a sure path to financial destruction.

From: *[XXXXXX]@unissula.ac.id*

Subject: *Concealed Business Proposition*

Date: *January 19, 2012 7:51:29 AM GMT-06:00*

To: *undisclosed-recipients*

Reply-To: *[XXXXXX]@zing.vn*

MR. SUNG LEE

DAH SING BANK LTD

DES VOEUX RD.BRANCH, CENTRAL HONG KONG,

HONG KONG.

Good Day,

I am Mr. Sung Lee, Auditing and Account Credit Officer, Dah Sing Bank Ltd (Hong Kong).

I do insist in your confidence in this transaction. I am making this contact with you, based on reliable information available to me courtesy of Internet business index and confirmed by my local chambers of commerce and industry concerning your reputation. Thus I am convinced you would be capable to provide me with a solution

---

to a money transfer transaction of Forty Three Million, Six Hundred Thousand United State Dollars. This is to seek your cooperation, as my foreign partner and your assistance to enable me own a property and invest in the stable economy of your country. Accept my apologies if this mail does not suit your personal or business ethics.

All other information to facilitate the remittance of the funds will be revealed to you in due course. For your assistance, you shall receive 25% of the funds to be transferred and 10% will be set aside for all expenses incurred by both parties. I will appreciate if you can reply me.

Kindly delete this e-mail if it does not suit your personal or business ethics, as I will gladly appreciate.

Yours faithfully,

Mr. Sung Lee

The above email is riddled with poor grammar and choppy sentence structure, but a reader would find that acceptable since it supposedly comes from Hong Kong. As you will notice, the email does not ask the reader to divulge any specific information. It simply asks the recipient to reply to the email if interested. It's impossible to predict what clicking the Reply and Send buttons would unleash.

Perhaps it would open a steady correspondence that builds trust and tries to forge a relationship between reader and writer before asking for bank account numbers. On the other hand, it could present a more immediate and direct danger by establishing a reverse link between receiver and sender. Or maybe the sender could hack into the recipient's computer and obtain enough information to clean out their bank accounts and steal their identification.

DOING UNTO OTHERS...

Spammers and scammers don't target individuals with just great job offers, crooked job offers or other amazing offers to flesh out their bank account. Scammers are nothing if not creative. They know that a large number of people would sacrifice their own comfort for the greater good: people who want nothing more than to help others. And so these con artists repeatedly come up with ideas on how to exploit that good-natured individual whose heartstrings are tugged by an email asking for their help, even if the individual sending the request is a stranger. The following email uses clever techniques to touch the hearts of what television icon Archie Bunker would call the "bleeding-heart liberals" among us.

From: [XXXXXX]@aol.com

Subject: Greetings!!!

Date: January 19, 2012 7:13:02 PM GMT−06:00

Reply-To: [XXXXXX]@yahoo.co.uk

Greetings

I am Mrs. Elena Hertz a citizen of Germany. I was married to Late Luis Hertz of blessed memory, since his death I have been battling with both Cancer of the lungs and fibroid problems.

While he was alive, he deposited a substantial amount of money worth Twelve Million Great Britain Pounds (£12,000,000.00) with a Financial Institution here in the United Kingdom which I inherited after his death.

I was made to understand by my medical experts that two month to live due to my unfortunate ailment.

I decided to hand over these funds to a devoted (God) fearing individual that will utilize this money for charity purpose and to help the needy the way i am going to instruct therein.

My dreams will rest on your shoulders when i receive your confident response in my private E-mail: [XXXXXX]@yahoo.co.uk

Remain bless

Mrs Elena Hertz

Email: [XXXXXX]@yahoo.co.uk

Who wouldn't want to be entrusted to work on a problem like the one explained in this email? I mean, really, how can anyone argue against such a lovely request? The writer of this email is

smart—"Elena" wrote the email to appeal to empathetic hearts everywhere. Regardless where you fall in the "faith" spectrum, from secular humanism, to Buddhism, to the mysteries of the Hindu faith, to Judaic-Christian philosophies, almost without exception, religion and philosophic thought stress the importance of reaching out to help someone in need. Add to this the consideration that people don't have to belong to a specified faith to be susceptible to these types of emails, and it's no wonder they are so commonplace.

But for argument's sake, let's look at the email a little more closely. Faith considerations aside, take a moment to think about the message. First, the email introduces its alleged author, putting a name and a face to the person behind the message. This gives the reader a name and place as well as a circumstance to consider when reading on. Like any good work of fiction, the writer provides the reader with a "character" they can empathize with—to some degree, we can all relate to illness and loss.

Using this method of approach, the master manipulator tugs at the heartstrings of unsuspecting and caring people. Not only are the gut-wrenching situations of illness and death exploited, but the writer has also made the wealthy character a martyr during the last days of her life by giving her a mission to share her millions with charity and the needy. And if that wasn't enough to make the reader warm up to this lovely lady, the writer strokes the reader's ego by pointing out their own "God fearing" qualities and suggesting they were divinely chosen to follow through with this woman's wishes.

Don't allow your curiosity to get the better of you.

This Is Your Lucky Day!

We've all heard stories about downtrodden individuals who, try as they might, never manage to catch a break, until suddenly, they come into an inheritance left by some long-forgotten relative. One such story tells how Hungarian brothers Zsolt and Geza Peladi spent the better part of their lives homeless and abandoned by their mother when suddenly charity workers tracked them down. The pair was discovered living in a cave outside of Budapest when they learned they would be sharing a $7 billion fortune with their sister, who lived in America.

A more bizarre tale involves Portuguese aristocrat Luis Carlos de Noronha Cabral da Camara. This man's story has been well documented by news agencies around the world and held up as an example of how not to divvy up your estate. Thirteen years before his death, Luis chose 70 names at random from the Lisbon telephone directory to inherit his estate. He didn't know any of the individuals he named in his will, and many were quite suspicious of their luck when they were told they were recipients of the man's wealth.

As they say, truth *is* stranger than fiction. Stories like this do happen. And that's why when confidence tricks like the Nigerian 419 scam—so-named because the first flood of these types of emails originated from Nigeria—targeted inboxes around the world in the early 1980s, people were anxious to believe they were among the lucky few touched by lady luck.

But remember, the house always wins—and that is true without fail when receiving an email like the following "Good News" example.

From: [XXXXXX]@chambers.com

Subject: GOOD NEWS

Date: January 13, 2012 4:28:17 AM GMT-06:00

Reply-To: [XXXXXX]@hotmail.co.uk

THE WILL HAS BEEN EXECUTED

Barristers' Chambers

Row Fred and Association

20 Great Sutton Street,

London WC1JH, England

LONDON - UK.

Attention: Beneficiary,

On behalf of the Trustees and Executor of the estate of Late Eng. Gregory Rims. I once again try to notify you as my earlier letter was returned undelivered. I hereby attempt to reach you again by this same email address on the WILL. I wish to notify you that late Gregory Rims made you a beneficiary in his WILL. He left the sum of Thirty Million Dollars ($30,000.000.00 US Dollars) to you in the Codicil and last testament to his WILL.

This may sound strange and unbelievable to you, but it is real and true. Being a widely traveled man, he said he met you sometime in past or simply you were nominated to him by one of his numerous friends abroad who wished you good,

I am not too sure again. Gregory Rims until his death was a member of the Helicopter Society and the Institute of Electronic & Electrical Engineers and a German property magnate. He was a very dedicated Christian who loved to give out aids to the poor, hungry and needy. His great philanthropy earned him numerous awards during his life time. Late Gregory Rims died on the 13th day of December, 2008 at the of 80 years, and his WILL is now ready for execution after 4 years and thorough investigations.

According to him, this money is to support your humanitarian/medical activities and to help the poor and the needy in our society. Please if I reach you as I am hopeful, endeavor to get back to me as soon as possible to enable me conclude my job. I hope to hear from you in no distant time.

I await your prompt response and please keep this very discrete and to yourself until the transfer of the funds to you is finalized.

Yours in Service,

Barrister Row Fred.

The sentiment behind the "Good News" email might tempt the recipient to click Reply. But if you pause for a moment and closely look at the message, it's hard to miss that it sounds like the email was written by an author whose first language was not English. Regardless what you'd like to believe about an email like this one, think objectively for a moment: this legal establishment appears to be based in London, England, and assuming most lawyers are educated and capable individuals with equally capable staff, a poorly constructed message like this one wouldn't see the light of day.

The next email example ("Congratulation!") promises another kind of windfall and tries to trick the reader by tossing out the name of the international organization, the United Nations Security Council. Addressing the issue of Internet fraud and email scams upfront reinforces the importance of the communication. Normal being normal, most of us would think that this message had to be legitimate because a criminal wouldn't address the topic of his or her criminal exploits so openly. But again, look at the poorly constructed message. Moreover, ask yourself how likely it would be that the United Nations Security Council would want to contact you in the first place. And finally, notice how this email makes no bones about asking directly for all the reader's personal information. This email screams an attempt at identity theft.

> *From: [XXXXXX]@secretshopper.com*
>
> *Subject: Congratulation! Congratulation! Congratulation!*
>
> *Date: January 17, 2012 11:44:58 AM GMT-06:00*
>
> *Reply-To: [XXXXXX]@yahoo.com*
>
> *The United Nations Security Council, hereby receives your payment with reference number #.*

MAV/UNO/WBO/LM-05-371 amounting to $800,000.00 (Eight Hundred Thousand dollars only)

This council was set up to fight against scam and fraudulent activities worldwide, responsible for investigating the legitimacy of unpaid contract, inheritance and lotto winning claims by companies and individuals and directs the paying authorities worldwide to make immediate payment of verified claims to the beneficiaries without further delay, your said payment was deposited with Financial Element FX Bank and you will gain online access for you to access and transfer your funds through internet banking, we also confirmed that you have met all statutory requirements in respect of your pending payment except that you have to change the name on the account which we opened for you with your funds, presently the name on the account is UNITED NATIONS so you need to change it to your name.

This important notice is to let you know that your payment is ready to be moved by Financial Element FX Bank Online banking transfer system where the account was opened.

All you are to do now is to contact United Nation director of Special Duties

To forward you all the necessary document.

Please note you will not be able to transfer your funds until you change the name on the account so you are to contact United Nation director of Special Duties with your information's as needed below.

(1) Your Full Name:

(2) Home Address:

(3) Phone, Fax and Mobile Number:

(4) Company Name/Occupation:

(5) Bank Name:

(6) Valid Copy OF Your Driving License

Here are the contact details of United Nation director of Special Duties which you are to contact immediately for your online account information's to confirm the availability of your funds.

NAME: Jessica EXCEL.

EMAIL: [address of recipient was included here]

You have to try to contact them as soon as possible so they can send you the online account information's as we have already informed them that you will be contacting them for the request of the account information's, please do not forget to contact them with your details as your request might be ignored if your information's is not included to prove that the message is coming from you.

Once Again Congratulation!!!

Yours Faithfully,

United Nations Security Council

And finally, to round out this portion of email scams, there's the typical "You Just Won the Big One" email. Again, winning the lottery doesn't happen to everyone either. But it does happen.

With that in mind, a reader desperate for cash might argue the email below sounds plausible. Why wouldn't your email be one of 12 pulled to participate in a draw? Somebody's got to win, right? In fact, the email sounds a little like the sweepstake that marketers such as Reader's Digest lottery mailings that have flooded snail-mailboxes everywhere for as long as most of us can remember. They are legitimate…aren't they?

But before rushing off to try to claim your prize, consider this: you have a one in 14 million odds of winning the Lotto 6/49. Slim pickin's if you ask me. According to a CBC report from 2009, you are "10 times more likely to die after being bitten by a poisonous snake or lizard" than winning the lottery. These are good facts to have tucked away in the back of your mind if you receive emails like the example below.

From: *espnstardptee@[XXXX].eu*

Subject: *YOUR EMAIL ACCOUNT HAVE WON 700,000.00 POUNDS IN ESPN CRICKET GLOBAL LOTTERY AWARD PROMOTION*

Date: *January 12, 2012 10:57:50 AM GMT-06:00*

To: *undisclosed-recipients*

Reply-To: *espnstardpte@pXXXX].eu*

ESPN CRICKET GLOBAL LOTTERY AWARD PROMOTION

ESPN CRICKET CENTER, LONDON

SE17NA-UNITED KINGDOM

PHONE:+447010045426

FAX:44+7006-034-185

MOTTO: STRIVING TO ALLEVIATE POVERTY ACROSS THE GLOBE

Payment No. M30911

YOU HAVE WON 700.000.00 POUNDS

YOU HAVE BEEN ANNOUNCED AS ONE OF THE 12 TOP LUCKY WINNERS ESPN CRICKET PROMOTION NEW YEAR AWARD 2012 !!!

Your Email account is randomly selected as one of the 12 top winners accounts who will get cash prizes from us. We are happy to inform you that you have won a prize money of (SEVEN Hundred Thousand British Pounds (700.000.00 GBP) lottery win promotion which is organized by UK /ASIA

ESPN CRICKET PROMOTION AWARD NEW YEAR 2012 WAS collects from the E-mail addresses of the people that are using especially yahoo mail, Gmail, sify mail, rediffmail,msn mail ,hotmail online and offline on messenger, among the millions that subscribe to internet we only select 12 people as our winners through electronic balloting System without the winner applying, we are congratulating you for been one of the people selected to receive top cash prize. All participant were selected through a computer balloting system drawn from Nine hundred thousand E-mail addresses from Canada, Australia, United States, Asia, Europe, Middle East, Africa and Oceania as part of our international promotions program which is conducted UK THIS NEW YEAR 2012.

This Lottery was promoted and sponsored by a conglomerate of some multinational companies as part of their social responsibility to the citizens in the communities where they have operational base.

Further more your winning details (e-mail address) to fiducial agent, as indicated in your play coupon and your cash prize of (700.000.00 GBP) will be released to you from this regional branch office .

We hope with part of your prize, you will participate in our end of year high stakes for 37 Million GBP international draw.

HOW TO CLAIM YOUR PRIZE

These are your Winning Information and Identification Numbers:

Reference Number...................... 02-0H-08

Ticket/Lotto Number 577-744-3465-E77

Batch Number 0952-K

File Number....................... FA-1305U-ID

Serial Number......................... 652-662

Category......................2ND CATEGORY

****

To begin your claims, kindly contact

Our Asian Fiduciary Agent

EMAIL ADDRESS BELOW ,

espnstardpte@XXXX.eu

DR. SMITH COLE (Fiduciary Agent)

****

You are required to forward your winning details via the above e-mail addresses. And note that you must sendion purposes.

1. FULL NAME...................................

2. COUNTRY OF ORIGIN ....

3. PRESENT ADDRESS............................

4. AGE..

6. SEX..

7. MOBILE NUMBER..............................

8. MARITAL STATUS.............................

9. BATCH NUMBER...............................

10. TICKET/LOTTO NUMBER ....

11. SERIAL NUMBER.............................

12. REFERENCE NUMBER..........................

13. CATEGORY..................................

14. AMOUNT WON................................

As soon as you contact the Fiduciary Agent, he will advise you on what to do in order to get your prize money.

> **APPROVED**
>
> **MR.PETERSON PAUL**
>
> **(CO-ORDINATOR)**

The next email example directly asks for money and promises big returns if you're willing to gamble with Club VIP Casino. The message appears direct in its purpose, and if an avid gambler received it, he or she might be tempted to check it out.

Online gambling isn't new; it provides individuals with a full range of gaming options, especially for people living in remote areas or with limited mobility. That's why an email like this example is especially dangerous—it seems believable. Sure, it promises better than average chances to win, but what gaming organization doesn't? Casino slot machines flash bright lights with similar messages promising a pot of gold if you insert your cash in that particular machine. And when asked, most people would admit they know they are taking a chance inserting that $20 bill.

Again, don't let yourself be deceived. These types of email are no more legitimate than the one naming you as a long-lost heir in line to receive millions of dollars.

From: *[XXXXXX]@am1500.com*

Subject: *Your quest for gaming glory fulfilled at Club VIP Casino*

Date: *January 11, 2012 9:24:43 AM GMT-06:00*

To: *[address of recipient was included here]*

The shortcut to gaming wealth begins with a 777 US dollars signup bonus with us and ends with our patrons striking extreme riches.

You can, too!

You'll be spoilt for choice at Club VIP with our more than 120 games to choose from and innovative bonuses.

Our promotions, like "Crack the Code" are open to all and a fun way to win substantial money to play with.

Our customer service and support team has earned well-deserved accolades.

Come over and you'll stay back to win and then win some more.

At this point, the email ends abruptly, without the usual pleasantries, but it does include a website address to click on and carry you away, presumably into gambler's heaven. Why, you might ask, would anyone fall for the email, or for any of these scams for that manner? The reality is that there are enough individuals who, against all reason, click the wrong button or provide thieves with the information they are looking for.

In a 2010 study, fraudulent activity, which includes these email scams, cost Canadians an estimated $10 billion each and every year. Considering that the Canadian Anti-Fraud Centre (CAFC) "shut down 45,000 email accounts being used by scammers..." it's a good bet that some of that billion-dollar loss can be contributed to email fraud.

AN OFFER YOU CAN'T REFUSE

And now for a look at an offer that looks like it might provide an honest income, but is more apt to get you into trouble than pad your bank account.

I'm probably the best example of a personality that, at one point in my life, might have fallen for the following seemingly harmless job offer. As a young stay-at-home mother, I was forever on the lookout to earn some extra money. And because so many advertisements offered work-from-home jobs, either in the classified sections of newspapers or glossy national magazines, the email from Costa Coffee Canada might have been an opportunity I would have considered following up on.

From: COSTA COFFEE CANADA

costacoffeecanada@[XXXXX].com

Subject: JOB OPPORTUNITY

Date: February 18, 2012 3:31:16 AM MST

To: undisclosed-recipients

Reply-To: www.[XXXX].co.uk

Dear Sir/Madam,

I am the Employment Manager of Costa Coffee, a quality coffee company based in the United Kingdom. The company has been setup in Lambeth, London since 1971, supplying all local caterers, major Italian and American coffee shops and around the world, with an exciting coffee, slow-roasted the Italian way. People couldn't get enough of it and by 1978 the first Costa espresso bar opened in Vauxhall Bridge Road in London.

To this day we still use the same method of slow-roasting our coffee beans, serving the brothers' authentic blend of 6 Arabic beans to 1 Robusta in 500 coffee shops all over the world. You can check out our website. We are looking for a representative in Canada who will be working for the company as a Part-Time Representative/Bookkeeper and we'll be willing to pay every week, of course it wouldn't affect your present state of work because you may do it as a PART-TIME work, all we need is just someone

*who would help us receive payments from our cus-
tomers in Canada. It wouldn't cost you any
amount. You are to receive payments, which will
be mailed to you by post from our customers in
Canada.*

*If you are interested, please fill the form below
and get back to me as soon as possible.*

Tom Nelson

costacoffeecanada@[XXXXX].com

COSTA COFFEE APPLICATION FORM

First Name:

Last Name:

Full Address (not p.o Box):

City:

State:

Zip:

Home Phone:

Mobile Phone:

Regards,

Tom Nelson

Costa Coffee,

Exporters of Quality Coffee.

www.[XXXX].co.uk

In this case, where a company looks like it wants to expand into another country, you might argue the legitimacy of a mass email meandering through Canadian cyberspace. But again, take a closer look at the text itself. As an employment manager allegedly based in the UK, Mr. Nelson isn't much of a writer. The email is riddled with grammatical errors—it's almost as if English isn't this gentleman's first language.

Also, note the extensive requests for personal information, which a legitimate employer might ask for. However, the writer of the email makes a request that is out of the ordinary. Nelson asks for a physical address; he specifically states he is not interested in a P.O. Box number because they don't provide the actual residence where the individual can be reached, which is usually necessary for potential creditors.

SMOKE AND MIRRORS

Perhaps the most disturbing example of an email scam that might have worked is a phony job offer that a colleague of mine received. The email seemed to target her specifically. The offer allegedly came from a Pastor Richard Taylor of Victory Church in the United Kingdom. Pastor Taylor explained that his church was hosting a women's conference and one of their key speakers had to cancel. Was it possible, Taylor asked my colleague, if she would consider travelling to London to take that speaker's place?

Because my colleague is a well-established Christian writer who has attended countless speaking engagements in numerous locations, the email request didn't seem too far-fetched. But she's a mystery writer—so she naturally checked it out.

She clicked on to the link provided, which took her to a website that reinforced the information in the email. There it was: Victory Church, Pastor Richard Taylor, and the site even provided information on the upcoming conference. My colleague's responsibilities were fairly minimal for the stipend she was being promised—$8500 USD for a two-hour speaking commitment. Also included in the offer were her flight and accommodations.

It was a wonderful opportunity, if it was indeed verifiable. Not only would my colleague add to her resume and her pocketbook, but she'd also be partaking in a once-in-a-lifetime experience. And despite the generous payment offered, it wasn't completely out of scope as far as speaking fees went. Still, doubts continued to tug at her heart; she needed a second opinion.

For added assurance, my colleague asked her husband to check out the offer. Who would better know if the request was a legitimate than a successful long-time business owner? When he too gave his nod to the deal, my writer friend signed and returned the attached contract and waited for further instructions she would receive by phone.

It was that much-anticipated telephone call that gave away this crook's scam. The thick South African accent sported by a gentleman claiming to be from Victory Church got my already suspicious friend more suspicious. Where was the Welsh accent, she wondered?

"I Googled 'Victory Church' and when I went to the website, low and behold, they had a different email and phone number," she explained in an email to other writers on a Canadian listserv.

"I emailed them right away and received a reply…stating that this was a scam and the Fraud Agency in London (UK) was investigating."

This victim then contacted the Fraud Squad in England and the RCMP, providing detailed information from the email she received and her telephone conversation in the hope of narrowing in on the perpetrators of this scam.

The RCMP officer my colleague dealt with explained that she was one of a very few who didn't lose money to these scammers. For those who did take the bait, the scammers can "end up with $2500.00 of the money they supposedly send you as an advance and they end up with enough information to duplicate your passport and identity."

My colleague later learned the website address provided in the email linked her to a "mirror website." There was indeed a Victory Church in the UK, but it had no connection whatsoever with the email she received.

Although it would have been wonderful to travel to London to do a job she loved for a great wage and all expenses paid, my colleague can't lament her change in fortune too much. She's grateful she didn't follow the opportunity further, and instead connected with the right people who were able to protect her from additional exposure to these conniving criminals. Had she continued to follow through with the offer, the result could have been more far-reaching than any mystery plot she could conjure up.

Every week scammers produce another twist to these old job-offer scams. Another attempt at targeting housewives or shut-ins was recently circulated by a company claiming the name "Eastern

Technology Ltd." It offered individuals as much as $1000 for as little as three hours of work per week. The individual applying for the position had to have access to the Internet and the ability to receive and "process checks at your local financial institution." From there, 90 percent of that money would be forwarded to a bank specified by the company, and the remaining 10 percent would be retained by the employee as payment for their services.

The obvious question is why these cheques aren't immediately deposited into the specified account. And if a person Googled "Eastern Technology," they'd find "Eastern Technology Corp." and "Eastern Technology Inc.," with little to no information on both companies. A little further down the Google results is mention of "Eastern Technology Ltd." with a scam warning beside it. Again, the message here is to research before responding to any offer, regardless how legitimate it might sound. A simple search will save you a lot of heartache in the long run.

AN ACT OF DESPERATION?

Most of us at one point or another have been at the end of our rope and hanging on to the last thread for dear life. All the overtime in the world doesn't seem to be paying the bills, and we find ourselves borrowing from one credit card to pay off another or using the nearest instant cash depot. Worse still, the utilities have been cut off and no one you know will give you a dime.

It's a desperate situation—the sort of scenario that one scammer considered when drafting the following email.

From: mrericterry@[XXXX].com

Subject: APPLY FOR LOAN @ 2% INTEREST

Date: March 23, 2012 1:15:09 AM GMT-06:00

To: undisclosed-recipients

Reply-To: mrericterry1@[XXXX].com

CREDIT LOAN SERVICE. Are you in need of financial help? Do you need a loan for your business, personal and investment loans to individual and companies to solve other monetary issues. We offer loans with a very low interest rate of 2%. Whatever your circumstances, self employed, retired, have a poor credit rating, we could

help Flexible repayment over for a minimum of 10 years, Interested applicants should submit their request via email (mrericterry1@[XXXX] .com) for immediate processing with the information listed below:

Names in full:

Address:

Gender:

Email:

Phone Number:

Amount Required:

Loan Duration:

Country:

We give out the following category of loan listed below:

```
=============================================
```

* *Platinum packaged loan ($30,000,000.00)*

* *Gold packaged loan ($20,000,000.00)*

* *Premium packaged loan ($10,000,000.00)*

* *Large Scale business loan ($1,000,000.00)*

* *Mortgage Loan ($500,000.00)*

* *Small scale business Loan ($200,000.00)*

* *Venture Capital ($100,000.00)*

* *Equipment Loan ($50,000.00)*

* *Consumer Loan ($30,000.00)*

* *Student Loan ($10,000.00)*

```
=============================================
```

In acknowledgment to these details, I will send you a well calculated Terms and Conditions for the amount you require.

Your faithful

Mr. Eric Terry

Again, ask yourself the logical questions if you receive an email similar to the "Apply for Loan" example. Would someone entrusted with offering the loans outlined above write such a poorly constructed email? What kind of businessperson offers the sums to individuals with whom they've had no prior connection? Is the two-percent interest rate reasonable?

It doesn't take much to see this for the scam it is, but a desperate person will often try anything. These scammers obviously hit their target demographic enough times to make these continued attacks profitable.

PROFILE OF A BELIEVER

A study coming out of Britain's University of Exeter in 2009 revealed a number of surprising statistics. Not only did researchers discover that 20 percent of the population of the UK was allegedly susceptible to some form of scams, but it also revealed the psychology of a victim of email fraud. According to the report, which was followed up by physorg.com, a research and technology news website, "previous victims of a scam [are] consistently more likely to show interest in responding again." Although the findings are representative of the population in the UK, this unique report provides a quick overview of situations quite likely mirrored in populations the world over:

- Scammers have been known to target individuals with whom they have some background knowledge. Particular targets are often people with interest in investing since an experienced investor might become a "victim through 'over-confidence.'"

- A typical victim profile isn't necessarily the elderly or vulnerable or individuals who are "poor decision makers." Instead, these victims "may have successful business or professional careers, but tend to be unduly open to persuasion by others and less able to control their emotions."

- According to a CBC news report, in 2005 "more than 200,000 Canadians [had] divulged personal information by responding to a phishing email." It was estimated that one in every 125 emails were a phishing attempt, and between three and five percent of recipients "take the bait."

- An estimated "5.7 million phishing emails are sent out worldwide every day."

These statistics are grim, but the picture darkens further when you consider that most victims of email scams don't tell anyone that they've been duped—a large percentage of victims keep their bad luck to themselves. Their worry about how to deal with a sudden financial loss is often overwhelming, damaging more than the person's bank account. Victims feel embarrassed they were "gullible enough" to fall for an email ploy, which is why many of them refrain from reporting their losses. But a quick reflection on the data below would suggest victims have no reason to feel embarrassed. Instead, they should feel angry at the increasing number of phishing expeditions flooding the Internet on a daily basis—and the growing number of victims who succumb to these emails, despite the ongoing attempt by authorities to educate the public against doing so:

- According to information collected and collated by the Canadian Anti-Fraud Centre in 2010, there were 17,055 documented cases of phishing schemes.

- Almost 3000 complaints were of suspected solicitation of information through the Internet, email or text messaging between July and September 2011.

• The CAFC noted a 78 percent increase in phishing schemes reported between January and the end of June 2011. The colours, logos and style of correspondence copied from most major banks were used to target victims, including the Royal Bank of Canada, Scotiabank, Canadian Imperial Bank of Commerce, Bank of Montréal and TD Canada Trust.

If you click on one of these emails, you may find yourself staring at what looks like a legitimate website on your browser. If someone knows what they're doing, it's not too difficult to write the software that will "spoof" or copy that webpage. If you type in any of your information, you risk having your bank accounts emptied and your identity stolen.

To avoid being scammed and giving your information to a con artist, open your Internet browser and type in your bank's URL directly. If there is a genuine problem with your account, you should find a message there informing you of this.

~

Chapter Five

Social Network Concerns

~

NOW WE'RE GETTING PERSONAL

The lines separating an obvious spam attempt to mine personal information and one to make a legitimate connection are blurred when someone contacts you through an email address you've made public in an effort to conduct a business transaction.

A prime example of this fraud comes out of Portage la Prairie, Manitoba.

On March 26, 2008, Portage resident Rob Hamilton approached his local RCMP about an odd email message he received from someone in the United Kingdom. The message was in response to an ad about a car Hamilton was selling on a local website. The individual responding to Hamilton's ad was willing to pay the man's asking price of $400, but the person went on to explain that they needed the vehicle shipped to the UK. Since the vehicle was inoperable and was advertised as strictly a parts vehicle, the entire correspondence was too bizarre for Hamilton to believe. What alarmed him more was the writer's request for Hamilton's personal information.

Hamilton didn't fall for what was to him an obvious scam. But his case made headlines in *The Portage Daily Graphic* as a warning to other residents who might not be as cautious as Hamilton had been. Portage RCMP Constable Dave Higgs warned residents to use caution with any email correspondence and to refrain from giving out any personal information, even in a case like Hamilton's, where he was trying to sell something online.

"They [con artists] have you on the hook because you want to sell something, so you want to provide them with this information, but if they are legitimate people, they will not ask for that (personal) information," Higgs told reporters.

Although most of us might be able to spot the danger behind many of the email examples discussed in this chapter, all common sense goes out the window when an email looks like it might have come from a friend or acquaintance. The writer of the following email used the name of an individual who was distantly connected to the book I wrote, *Missing! The Disappeared, Lost or Abducted in Canada*. Because of that, I couldn't help but wonder, what if my friend really was stranded and I ignored her plea for my help?

From: *[XXXXXX]@yahoo.ca*

Subject: *Just Robbed in Madrid*

Date: *January 26, 2012 12:34:05 PM GMT-06:00*

To: *undisclosed recipients*

Reply-To: *[XXXXXX]@yahoo.ca*

I hope you get this on time, I am in Madrid Spain at the moment and I just had my bags stolen with my passport and personal effects therein. I am here for a conference and I lodged in a Hotel and when I left for dinner I returned to find out that my things where stolen without the door of my room broken, I guess someone had a key and stepped in when I was out. I have reported the case to the hotel management and the local police here, the case is being investigated at the moment but I don't feel safe here anymore so I plan to move to another hotel soon while the case is being investigated. I am currently using the hotel Internet service to reach you, I have been to the embassy here and they got me a temporary travel passport but I need some cash to take care of some expenses as my money was stolen with my bag. I have made contact with my bank but it would take me 3 working days to access funds in my account from Madrid.

I would love you to assist me and I will refund as soon as I can access funds from my account I am thinking Western Union transfer is the best option to send money to me. Let me know if you need my details (Full names/location) to make the transfer. You can reach me via email or the hotel's desk phone +34962463149.

Let me know if you can be of any help.

Gladys R****

Gladys' plea for help is an Internet rendition of the "emergency" or "grandparent" scam. This ploy will be examined in the telephone scam section of this book. At this point, suffice it to say that the psychology behind this email is to create immediate concern that is quickly followed by a knee-jerk reaction. The goal is to get the recipient to send money first and analyze the request later. By then, of course, it's too late to do much about any money already sent.

It has been a while since I'd received an email purporting to be from a friend or acquaintance of mine. The first time this kind of "emergency" correspondence appeared in my inbox, I was tempted to follow through on the request for help, but the email was from a distant acquaintance so I didn't take it seriously.

How was an identity thief or fraudster able to send this email to me? Was my friend the original target or was I, or—more likely—were both of us? And how on earth did the fraud artist connect us?

Since email scammers attack in bulk, it stands to reason that the writer of the email randomly collected addresses from websites, social networks and other sources containing Gladys' name and fanned out emails to thousands of people, not only to the individuals who had some contact with the woman. Additionally, it's more likely that Gladys' email account was hacked, and the cyber thief collected the contact information from that angle.

But there might be another possibility. Perhaps the perpetrator accessed a website that publicized the personal information of millions upon millions of individuals worldwide, providing a field day for potential identity thieves everywhere.

Chances are pretty good that you or someone you know has a connection to an information goldmine.

It's called social media.

THE DANGERS OF SOCIAL NETWORKS

One of the immediate wonders of the Internet and email technology in particular is their ability to connect people around the world. Family members separated by oceans and continents can now communicate with each other instantly, instead of waiting for sometimes weeks before getting a response to a letter.

Building on the instant connection the Internet afforded, it wasn't long before the first attempts at social networking hit the information highway. GeoCities was among the first such networks. Founded by David Bohnett and John Rezner in 1994, GeoCities offered users a choice between one of six cities to connect with and establish their own web pages. These "cities" or online "neighbourhoods" were named Colosseum, Hollywood, RodeoDrive, Sunset-Strip, WallStreet and WestHollywood, and users chose their "neighbourhoods" by the themes they were affiliated with. For example, SiliconValley, a neighbourhood added during one of GeoCities' original expansions, had a computer-related theme. This first attempt at social networking was successful, if somewhat complicated. And in January 1999, Yahoo purchased GeoCities for $3.57 billion in stock.

Yahoo closed the North American branch of GeoCities in 2009. By then, other networking sites were gaining enormous popularity, building on the experience of their predecessors. Friend-ster (2002) and MySpace (2003) continued to push the envelope further, honing in on users' desire to make and build friendships, and sites like LinkedIn offered a tech-savvy opportunity to expand business relationships.

And then there was Facebook.

Launched in 2004, Facebook grew rapidly and universally in ways that Mark Zuckerberg and his colleagues never dreamed possible at the time. And while today Facebook is one of several options for individuals to make connections around the globe, it remains one of the most popular.

According to Facebook's company history, about 845 million people use the site every month. About 80 percent of that number are "monthly active users…outside the U.S. and Canada." In addition, as of December 2011, there were more than "425 million monthly active users who use Facebook mobile products." Add to these figures the number of people who also patronize such sites as LinkedIn—which in 2011 boasted 100 million professionals world-wide—and the information highway has truly succeeded in developing a global community like no other.

Perhaps one of the biggest factors in the success of social networking sites like Facebook is the simple and direct approach they use to assist in connecting people. Any personal data you want to share with friends, family or new acquaintances can be included in the information section of your Facebook page. Photos, interesting activities, trips, jobs, loves and breakups—you can inform the important people in your life about all this and more with a quick update on your profile, and the individuals on your friend list will receive that information in nanoseconds.

Of course, this ease of access to personal information has also provided criminals with a mammoth database to work with—an absolute gold mine for identity thieves.

YOUR ID—FOR SALE OR RENT...EVEN ON FACEBOOK?

Ever notice how the ads appearing on your Facebook pages almost always reflect your interests in some way? While you might not bite at any of these offers, they get your curiosity going. For example, the ads that typically appear when I'm on Facebook have to do with faith issues, exercise, yoga or writing—all topics dear to my heart.

In the writing of *Missing! The Disappeared, Lost or Abducted in Canada* and *Unsolved Murders in Canada*, I became involved in several Facebook groups. This involvement expanded until I acquired hundreds of friends on my personal Facebook friend list who were otherwise unknown to me. Because I don't know most of these people aside from Facebook, I've maintained limited information about myself online. However, enough information is there for advertisers to target me. All you have to do is "Like" a Facebook page and a potential advertiser has another clue to your preferences. If this information gives advertisers enough to work with when building an advertising program, there's no telling what can happen if criminals target your site.

To demonstrate this theory, I only need to remind you of the emergency email request I received from my acquaintance Gladys. Like many of the people on my friends list, I've only ever connected with Gladys through Facebook.

The Entrepreneurs' Organization (EO) addressed the safe use of social networks in an online article to its roughly 8000 members. It points out how Facebook status updates, such as a trip you are taking or an evening meeting, could leave you vulnerable to criminal attacks. And that when it comes to identity theft, the "use of photo- and video-sharing sites like Flickr and YouTube provide deeper insights into you, your family and friends, your house, favourite hobbies and interests."

While most of us know it's bad practice to share our Social Insurance Number, EO also suggests that profile information, such as your full name, your birth date, your home town, the schools you attended, even your hobbies and other interests, all put you at risk with identity thieves. These small bits of data can flesh out a person's life and offer hints to the user's Facebook password—how many times have you used your mother's maiden name as a password? Information like the pieces stated above open the door to potential phishing expeditions, such as the "emergency" email I received. These phishing expeditions can be used to gain your confidence and engage you in online discussions with the sole purpose of acquiring more personal data.

Aside from targeting your identity directly, if you have an application associated with your Facebook profile, you run the risk of exposing your computer to viruses and malware, another term for malicious software. According to OE, "Ninety-five percent of

Facebook profiles have at least one application, many of which are not reviewed and can be used for malicious and criminal purposes."

MSN Money, an American business news website associated with the cable television business news channel CNBC, further heightened concerns over online social networking when it published an article in October 2011 that targeted Facebook's Timeline feature. The new feature provides increasingly detailed personal information that, as the article states, "doesn't have monetary value for Facebook users, but it does for marketers—and criminals," two groups who are "especially drawn to social media to gain access to consumers."

That doesn't mean we should all delete our accounts on Facebook and other social media sites. But it does mean we need to be especially careful what we share on those sites. Aside from limiting personal information, here are a few additional best practices suggested by several sources, including those listed by the Entrepreneur's Organization:

- Never provide private information, such as your Social Insurance Number, on a social network site or to anyone other than a potential employer.

- Protect your username and password with the same vigilance you protect your bank card and password.

- Change your passwords on a regular basis.

- Despite the desire to reach out and meet new people, OE suggests you only invite people you know on to your friends list.

With that in mind, sites like Facebook can continue to provide a vehicle for maintaining connections. You might want to think carefully, though, about what you include on your profile if you plan to use it to increase exposure for other reasons, such as raising a business profile.

CHAIN LETTERS

This section wouldn't be complete without including one additional email scam that's been around for years and looks harmless enough—so much so that even the most vigilant paranoia among us has likely succumbed to its wiles. This email scam is the online version of the dreaded chain letter.

Chain letters have been around for centuries, and because of their unwieldy history it's hard to say exactly where the chain letter as we know it today began. Snopes.com, an Internet site that calls itself the definitive "reference source for urban legends, folklore, myths, rumors, and misinformation," dates the first official chain letter, which contained specific instructions to make copies for a certain number of recipients, to 1888. In some cases these letters contained folklore, urban legends, or recipes for healing potions. In other cases, the letters were used to generate a form of revenue. Some chain letters warned that if a recipient of the letter failed to follow through with the instructions it contained, some form of bad luck would befall them.

Chain letters aren't foreign to email users either. Almost as soon as people began using the Internet, chain mail started making the rounds. Chances are the email example supposedly from the

American Cancer Society might sound familiar to you. It has been credited with the dubious honour of being named the first email chain letter and has made its rounds since 1997.

> *Jessica Mydek is seven years old and is suffering from an acute and very rare case of cerebral carcinoma. This condition causes severe malignant brain tumors and is a terminal illness. The doctors have given her six months to live. As part of her dying wish, she wanted to start a chain letter to inform people of this condition and to send people the message to live life to the fullest and enjoy every moment, a chance that she will never have.*
>
> *Furthermore, the American Cancer Society and several corporate sponsors have agreed to donate three cents toward continuing cancer research for every new person that gets forwarded this message. Please give Jessica and all cancer victims a chance. Add ACS@[XXXX].COM to the list of people that you send this to so that the American Cancer Society will be able to calculate how many people have gotten this.*
>
> *If there are any questions, send them to the American Cancer Society at ACS@[XXXX].COM*
>
> *Three cents for every person that receives this letter turns out to be a lot of money considering how many people will get this letter and how many people they, in turn, pass it on to. Please go ahead and forward it to whoever you know—it really doesn't take much to help out.*

The problem is that the Jessica Mydek in this letter doesn't exist, and the American Cancer Society never had a program like the one mentioned to collect research money. Recipients who forward the letter to their friends and family feel that they've done something good, when in reality they have perpetrated a hoax that could tarnish the name of a well-respected organization.

If you've read through the rest of this chapter, you are aware of another concern. Without a second thought, many individuals who responded to the email and forwarded it to their friends and family members clicked on that forbidden link authorities warn us about. In doing so, they may have given the originator of the email access to the recipients' computers through a reverse link—this is similar to the link you may have initiated when you give a computer or Internet technician remote access to your computer to help repair a connection. Once that link is established, a criminal can access more of your personal information and even control your computer, turning it into a "zombie." From there, hackers can connect your computer to a network of other computers under their control, forming what's known as a "botnet."

As David Holtzman explains in his book, *How to Survive Identity Theft*, a botnet is "a group of compromised computers that can be launched en masse at a higher profile target, usually a computer belonging to a company or government agency." Despite increased security, these computers can be "broken into either by 'cracking' the encryption using 'brute force' (trying every reasonable option) or by a massed attack that overwhelms their defenses."

This is identity theft of a different nature. Holtzman says that "this kind of attack steals your computer's identity and uses it to commit crimes." Your computer might not be chosen to be part of a botnet, but such an attack can threaten the security of your private information and, in turn, threaten your identity and your resources.

Renditions of the Jessica Mydek email have circulated around the world for more than a decade now. Sometimes the name of the main subject has been changed. Perhaps the circumstances are different or the location has been altered—let's face it, we're all more likely to help out when the little girl or boy involved lives close by and the organization benefitting from our efforts is local.

Once again, the moral of the story remains the same. If you read an email that is sapping too much of your mental energy, check out its authenticity. Make direct contact with the authority listed in the message. Do not click on any links in the email. Instead, type the website directly into the address bar on your browser. This will eliminate any concerns you have about the anonymous victim and will save you a lot of heartache in the process.

The wiser that email users become about the dangers of spam, the more clever spammers become in disguising their emails. Some businesses do connect with their clients via email and include direct links to websites within the emails. For example, I recently received emails from a credit card company I deal with, announcing I could win $1 million in credit should I respond to a survey; I've been informed that my domain name needs renewing; PayPal is once again begging me to review my account; and a stranger wrote a general email about her alleged bad luck with a spam email. In this last scenario, the woman was "warning" readers of how she was taken in by a scam and supplied a web link to a "government" site she claimed helped her recover her money. All of these emails included some type of link that claimed to speed along the request and limit the inconvenience to my time. And when legitimate companies such as mobile phone providers that notify you when your bill is ready, it's becoming increasingly difficult to determine what is legitimate and what is not.

Group listservs aren't exempt from the wiles of hackers, either. I've had emails from what looked like the legitimate email addresses of friends and acquaintances, suggesting I check out a link, only to have another email sent shortly after from that individual claiming they hadn't sent the first email.

Because it is impossible to ensure the links within emails don't connect to a bogus site looking to steal your personal information, the best rule of thumb is to delete any strange emails receive. If you don't have a reader window that allows you to read your mail without actually opening the email, contact the company some other way to request additional information on the email.

Furthermore, if you want to share a link with a friend to a page on the Internet, suggest they Google the topic rather than including the web address in your email. It's always better to be safe than sorry.

According to the Better Business Bureau, "almost half of [Canadians] shop online, we have about 13 million Facebook and 3.5 million Twitter accounts, and we send nearly five billion text messages each month." John Russo, vice president, legal counsel and chief privacy officer with Equifax Canada, points out that "because of this high degree of online activity, we are also susceptible to online fraud." With that in mind, the following checklist offers helpful need-to-know pointers on keeping your personal information safe when you venture on to the World Wide Web.

Online Safety Checklist in Review

- Have two email addresses. Use one for business and personal contacts you know well and trust, and use the second email address for additional online interactions, such as social network sites, for example.

- Never open or reply to unsolicited email. Opening a spam email can send a signal to the sender that he has connected with a working email address, which can open you up to further fraudulent attempts by that spammer.

- Pay careful attention to all your emails. If you subscribe to newsletters, chat groups or listservs connected with special interest groups, you could be targeted by a scam email that is dressed up to look like the one you usually get and are expecting. This is not unlike brand spoofing or phishing, where emails and text messages look like they come from the actual source—like the banking emails we've all found in our inbox at one time or another. But some of these imposters are harder to recognize than others, so if you're suspicious for any reason, such as a sender you've never heard of, check it out before responding.

- If your email program offers a full view of emails without officially opening them, and you think the correspondence appears official but leaves you suspicious, refrain from succumbing to whatever persuasive message you might find.

- If you're so troubled by an official-looking email that you can't stop thinking about it, telephone the business directly, or type in their web address directly into your browser's address bar.

- The RCMP advises people to never enter personal information on a web page that does not have a secure connection. A lock icon should be visible on either the lower or upper right corner of the web page, depending on the site and the browser.

- If you receive an "emergency" email from a friend or acquaintance, saying they're stranded and looking for money to get home, telephone the individual to check out the legitimacy of that email before responding to it

- Most legitimate emails should come from someone you know or have been in contact with. Therefore, ask yourself if you know the person before responding to the email.

- That being said, make sure any email *sounds* legitimate. If the subject or the content of the email strikes you as odd, think twice before responding to it. Instead, contact the individual who allegedly sent it to ensure that it was actually sent by someone you know. Contact should preferably be made in some way other than email in case that person's email address has been hacked into and your request is rerouted to the hacker.

- Never provide any personal information to an email request, even if it appears to come from a legitimate organization.

- Never email personal information, such as your Social Insurance Number or driver's licence number, to anyone, even if the request appears to come from a legitimate business contact. Email correspondence is not completely secure, and you never know when that email can be accessed by someone other than the intended recipient and used to strip you of your good name.

- Never use a public computer to do your banking or other private business.

- If you are using your own laptop on a public wireless network, make sure the establishment offering Wi-Fi has the appropriate security measures in place.

- Never click on any button option on pop-up ads—that includes the "Close" button. Clicking any button could install Spyware on your computer. Instead, click the "X" in the top right or left corner of the ad, or close your browser altogether and reboot.

- Never download anything from a site you are unfamiliar with. Installing games, toolbars and any type of software can open you up to potential viruses and, in some cases, identity theft.

- Change your passwords often—at least every three months. You might argue that you won't remember your password if you do that, but most websites provide retrieval options via email if you forget your password. However, if you do forget your password, and your password is emailed to you, that is a good time to change your password.

- Passwords should be at least eight characters long. Never choose common identifiers, such as your pet's name or your birth date as your password. Information like this is often readily available and, therefore, easy to figure out.

- Refrain from simply choosing a word as your password. Good dictionary software can have a cyber thief cracking your carefully chosen password in minutes. If you prefer to use a single word, consider misspelling it or inserting a number in it.

- One clever way to choose a password is to create a sentence and use the first letter in each word. For example: "I love spending my summers at the beach" becomes ILSMSATB.

- Only purchase items from online businesses that have a reputable track record that you can check out.

- Equifax Canada notes that when you hit the "Checkout" button when shopping online, "you should see a change in the Web address at the top of your browser. If the site you're shopping on is equipped with security layers, you should see 'http' change to 'https,' and you might also see a small padlock icon, depending on your browser."

- Make sure your home network is properly secured with encryption, such as Wi-Fi Protected Access (WPA), and do not allow unauthorized people to access your wireless network.

- Keep your anti-virus programs current.

- Turn off your wireless network when not in use.

- Be equally as vigilant with your cellphone as you are with your computer. The phishing attacks and spam messages sent to your computer can now be done through text messages, and the same precautions are necessary to keep you and your personal information safe on your cellphone or any other PDA. Unwanted text messages, whether they overtly ask for personal information or are subtler in their approach, can be used to garner personal details and potentially steal your identity.

It's crucial to be careful when conducting any kind of business online. But it's equally crucial that one doesn't become paranoid when using modern technology. Don't hide your head in the sand, thinking that because you don't shop or bank online, or because you don't participate in any of the various social networking groups, you won't fall victim to identity theft and identity fraud.

Believe it or not, lots of folks who never venture online have been victimized in this manner. Instead, educate yourself on new trends in fraud and consider embracing the Internet as part of your regular financial regimes. According to Equifax Canada, "consumers who frequently monitor their accounts online are most likely to uncover fraud the fastest."

Chapter Six

Mail Fraud

~

NEIGHBOURHOOD WATCH TAKES ON A WHOLE NEW MEANING

The protection of personal mail or valuable merchandise has been a longstanding challenge of distance communication since humankind first developed a written system of sharing information with individuals living outside one's home community. Lone messengers traversing great distances could meet with robbers anxious to intercept sensitive correspondence or relieve them of any valuables on their person.

In time, messengers travelled in pairs for safety reasons, and eventually mail delivery increased to more than a single, official dispatch and contained letters from the general public. In 1516 Britain established an official postal system, the Royal Mail, which in time initiated one of several stagecoach systems familiar throughout most of Europe and later, North America. According to some sources, these stagecoaches could travel between key locations at speeds of four to seven miles (6 to 11 kilometres) per hour. Larger amounts of mail could be transported, but of course that also meant a potentially greater haul should a robber target a particular mail coach.

Even at seven miles per hour and with a couple of armed men in attendance, the stagecoach system was not a foolproof method when it came to safe deliveries.

The safety of our mail has evolved in leaps and bounds since the Wild West days of the stagecoach. But despite the countless security measures initiated by postal systems around the world, snail mail is still fairly vulnerable. Think about it—before any document makes it from sender to intended recipient, it's passed through countless pairs of hands, sorted and stored potentially at several locations and transported over land and sea via truck, train, boat or plane. We place a lot of trust in our postal workers. Not only do they need to be reliable in the execution of their duties, but they also safeguard our mail. We need to trust that they're not going to make off with that cheque we're expecting from a business client or Revenue Canada.

Fortunately, the majority of our postal workers are as competent as they are trustworthy. But as with any industry, there are always exceptions. In June 2011, two postal workers in the Greater Toronto Area were charged with "stealing about $500,000 worth of goods that were being shipped through the mail." Peel Regional Police Constable Tim Ruttan told *Toronto Sun* reporter Chris Doucette that while the thieves "generally targeted gift cards...pretty much anything of monetary value was being stolen."

More recently, in February 2012, a 64-year-old female postal worker was arrested for "allegedly stealing gift cards." In this case Canada Post conducted its own investigation after workers noticed opened, damaged or missing packages. Canada Post said they had video surveillance "allegedly" showing suspicious behaviour involving this suspect, and when she was arrested, the woman had several gift cards in her possession.

Despite situations like the ones described above, the biggest threat to the safety of land mail comes from the fraud artists who make their living looking for ways to collect your money—and with it, your name. It takes the efforts of an entire neighbourhood to keep everyone safe, and that includes watching out for your neighbour's mail.

The news stories above depict a disturbing picture of the large number of individuals who are still fooled by letters promising untold riches. But sometimes all it takes is a new twist to an old theme for people to let their guard down, if only for a moment, and get caught up in something that will cost them dearly in the end.

In September 2011, Detective Sergeant Michael Egan of the London, Ontario, fraud unit voiced concerns to the media about a new mass mail-fraud con who spoofed an old email scam. The concern stemmed from a report by Dan Huggins, a London resident who received a letter claiming to be from a Malaysian woman named Rebecca Nadeem. The letter claimed that the writer was dying from terminal cancer, and her last wish was to do something wonderful with her $21.6 million fortune.

To that end, Nadeem said she would give 30 percent of her millions to Huggins if he promised to "build a charity organization for the saints and less privileged" in her name. If Huggins helped in this so-called mission of mercy, all he had to do was email Nadeem at the address she provided in the letter. As was reviewed in the Internet and email section of this book, once that connection was made, Huggins could have opened himself up to having his computer accessed and personal and financial information collected.

News Alert:
Traffic Stop Yields More than Vehicle Infraction

When Vancouver police officers pulled over a rental car in July 2011 for making a wrong turn, they uncovered several interesting bits of information.

To begin with, the 28-year-old Colombian national and Fort Lauderdale, Florida, resident Juan Hernandez didn't have a driver's licence. But that was small potatoes compared with the contents in the vehicle Hernandez was driving: several mailbags filled the front passenger seat.

Not just anyone is allowed to be in possession of mailbags and they certainly aren't supposed to be shipped around the country in unofficial vehicles.

As it turned out, Vancouver police had uncovered an international mail-fraud operation that spanned 10 countries and affected thousands of victims.

Because police were presented with the evidence staring at them from the front seat of the car, and because Hernandez pleaded to charges of "fraud over $5000," many of the details in this case came together rather quickly.

An examination of the contents of the mailbags uncovered cash and cheques from elderly victims in response to a mass mailout marketing fraud.

Victims between the ages of 68 and 94 were targeted with "letters from

Florida saying they'd just won $2 million or more, but they had to mail a $30 processing fee to Vancouver to claim the prize."

Equipped with a false identification, Hernandez set up four postal boxes where he would collect these remittances. Byron Chu of Quebecor Media Inc. (QMI Agency) reported that 200 such remittances were collected from just one of those mailboxes, and a "total of $20,000 in cash was seized in the investigation, and 5000 victims were identified," including one Canadian.

Mail scams of this scope set up operations out of many cities and countries and don't usually stay long in any one place before moving on to another location. The masterminds behind these kinds of crime also use geography to blur the connections between place and time and any fraudulent activity, should it become detected, making it difficult for the authorities to connect the dots and make an arrest.

"If I'm running a mass mailing scam I might do it out of Vancouver, but my mailboxes would be somewhere in the United States, maybe Texas, and my victims would probably be in England," Vancouver Police Detective Rick Stewart explained.

Another international scam was unveiled in Edmonton in October 2011 when a 39-year-old man in that city was arrested on charges of fraud and money laundering in relation to a "$7-million mail fraud scam."

CBC News reported that a cooperative effort between the RCMP, Canadian Postal Inspectors and officials from the U.S. Postal Service helped pinpoint the man who, in this case, was suspected of removing "more than 2200 mail items from both the U.S. and Canadian mail systems."

This international scam originated in Edmonton but mainly zeroed in on residents south of the border.

Once again, victims were told they had won money in a "consumer lottery." The clincher in this scam was that each "winning" recipient also received a cheque to "cover the cross-border fees related to redeeming their prize."

You can see where this is going by now, I am sure. The cheques were fraudulent. But the ruse fooled enough people that it was a lucrative con for the criminals, and a costly one for the victims who lost an average of $3600 each.

Because the letter looked "official," Huggins opened it as soon as he noticed it, thinking perhaps it came from a friend who might be travelling. But once he read its contents, he saw it for the scam it was.

Although he didn't fall for the letter's claims, Huggins was concerned that others, in particular seniors, might not be as cautious, especially since the writer of the letter he received targeted the elderly: "...I know that you are reliable and elderly person and my instinct tells me that you will carry out this project effectively. My instinct never failed me before and I am sure it will not fail me this time..."

The elderly are especially vulnerable when it comes to these kinds of scams, as well as mailings promising big windfalls. It's not because they're being greedy; it's quite the opposite in fact. Elderly folk are often worried about providing some type of financial comfort to their children and grandchildren—they want to receive money so they can help the ones they love.

Egan suggested the rise of Internet security and online awareness has pushed scammers to ply their pressure via snail mail. Of the thousands of letters potentially sent in a single scam, all the con artists need are "one or two people to bite" on the offer, Egan said.

Protecting yourself from falling victim to these offers is simple—stay away! Anyone telling you that you've won money but have to send money to claim your prize, which is often called a "Sweepstake Scam," isn't legitimate. If you need any convincing, consider this: Canadians do not pay taxes on the proceeds from a lottery win.

If you've received mail promising you a cash settlement for providing a service—completing a requested task, for example—report it to the local authorities. Your municipal or provincial police will be able to clarify whether the request has merit. Under no circumstances should you follow through on any part of a request—

even opening a simple email from an unknown source could compromise the security of your personal information.

LOCK UP YOUR MAILBOX!

While door-to-door mail delivery still exists in many parts of this country, the familiar image of a postal carrier braving the elements to deliver your daily mail is fast becoming obsolete. Although we will always require some form of land mail services, how those services are being provided is changing. In newer city developments, door-to-door service has been replaced with multi-family locked mailboxes; these community units are beginning to appear in older neighbourhoods as well. Cost-cutting measures, such as reducing the number of mail carriers, are most certainly a consideration. It's also one way to prevent mail theft.

Mail theft provides criminals with the possibility of collecting government cheques and gift cards, but it is also a low-tech method of committing identity theft. Think about it: mail carriers work during the day when most residents are at work or busy running errands. A thief can monitor your neighbourhood to see who's usually out during the day, follow a few minutes behind the mail carrier and then bag a lot of mail in a relatively short time. The thief can also collect names and addresses and is one step closer to stealing someone else's identity.

A prime example of criminals targeting mail in an identity-theft ring comes out of Edmonton in the summer of 2010. Mailboxes in 140 apartment blocks throughout the city were broken into and the mail stolen. Edmonton Detective Calvin Mah told Michelle

Thompson of the *Edmonton Sun* that the police investigation determined that the "mail was then used to commit identity theft and fraud."

According to Mah, breaking into the locked mailboxes was a simple task for these criminals. "Some of the surveillance images we were able to acquire showed they were able to get in and out within a minute," he told reporters. The villains were able to camouflage their tampering and returned several times until they were satisfied they had enough information on their victims to produce a believable profile. At that point they applied for credit cards and bank loans.

Several postal workers noticed the mailboxes looked as though they had been interfered with, and they alerted the authorities that something might be up. Without these postal workers' due diligence, many more Edmontonians could have fallen victim to this mail scheme. Nine people faced 100 charges in relation to this case.

Clearly, locking up your mail is important but not foolproof. Still, it's a pretty safe bet that if you receive mail directly at your front door, a thief is less apt to try to scoop it up if you have a mailbox that is locked. Canada Post community mailboxes are state-of-the-art, and while nothing is impossible, it's highly unlikely someone could break into them without being noticed.

Tax Time Is Prime Time for ID Thieves

Intercepting snail mail becomes an even bigger concern around tax season, when T4s and other tax documents loaded with personal information are mailed out. Tax season is a busy time for identity thieves who recognize that mail theft at this time of year is far more profitable than other times when it comes to collecting personal information they're looking for from home mailboxes. Along with a person's name, address, workplace and income, T4s contain that coveted piece of information all identity thieves are looking for—a Social Insurance Number.

In preparation for the increase in personal data flowing through mailboxes, some identity thieves have prepared in advance by filing change of address forms for the victims they target. This was admittedly easier to do before Canada Post initiated several safety features, such as requesting a valid email address, a Canadian phone number, credit card and government-issued identification to safeguard residents from potential identity thieves.

Still, identity thieves are vigilant and organized. If they target a specific neighbourhood, chances are they have been watching the area for some time and may have collected the personal information needed to carry out their plans. Steal a telephone bill and they have a resident's phone number. Intercept a pre-approved credit card application and fraud artists can get a new credit card. With these two pieces of information, identity thieves are well on the path to applying for a change of address—and collecting even more personal information. The entire process may be time consuming, but it is not impossible.

Another ruse that's been profitable to identity thieves in the past is distributing fake tax forms that appear as though they've come directly from Revenue Canada, complete with logos and all. These documents ask for additional information that has allegedly been missed from a filed return. Because this correspondence comes via land mail and appears legitimate, it's understandable that some residents comply with the requests and, inadvertently, become victims of identity theft. All too often the elderly make up the largest demographic of victims succumbing to this type of fraud.

In addition to traditional land-mail requests, official-looking emails allegedly sent by Revenue Canada have tricked people into divulging sensitive personal information. Although it's not uncommon for Revenue Canada to contact you through snail mail, just as financial institutions do, they will *never* contact you via email about your personal tax return, and they will never provide a link to click on for more information.

Due diligence is required to protect your private and sensitive information. Monitoring your land mail can't be emphasized enough. It is one more safety measure to keep identity thieves at bay.

MAIL SAFETY CHECKLIST

- Monitor your snail mail. If you suddenly find you are receiving less mail, this could indicate someone may be intercepting your mail in order to steal your identity. If your mail trickles to a near stop, this could signal that a mail thief has sent in a change of address form to the post office on your behalf.

- Never ship cash in the mail—that includes retail gift cards. Sending gift cards in the mail is like sending cash since anyone who gets their hands on the gift card can use it without any difficulty.

- Don't send brightly coloured envelopes in the mail: they are a clue the mail might have been sent in celebration of a special occasion and may contain a cheque, money or gift card.

- Keep a list of the utility and other bills you expect in the mail and the dates you expect them to arrive. If that date has passed, contact the issuer to find out if the bill has been sent.

- Don't send cheques in the mail. Pay your utility or other bills at the bank or online. If you absolutely must use snail mail, purchase a money order or send the payment via registered mail. This way, if your mail has been stolen, you will be aware of the interception.

- If you've ordered something that's being delivered in the mail, keep a record of that transaction, complete with the name and contact information of the company you're dealing with, the amount and method of payment and the expected date of delivery.

- Empty your mailbox daily, preferably as soon as it is delivered.

- If you plan to be away for any length of time, have someone pick up your mail for you. If you are away for an extended period of time and pick-up arrangements can't be made, consider having your mail temporarily redirected or put a hold on your mail and pick it up directly at the post office when you return.

- If your mail isn't delivered to a secured neighbourhood lock box, consider purchasing a personal locked mailbox.

- When sending mail, consider taking it directly to the post office. If that's not possible, check the pick-up times at portable mail-boxes and drop off your mail just before that scheduled time.

- Receiving mail addressed to someone else, especially when you've lived at a particular residence for a long time and haven't received mail for that individual before, could signal that you've become a victim of identity theft.

- Never accept or pay for merchandise you received through the mail that you hadn't ordered, even if it comes disguised as a "free gift." If you succumb to the lure of this proposal, you could live to regret it. Simply send it back at the sender's request.

- Home-improvement scams are also proliferated through the mail, as are job-offer and work-at-home schemes, as well as offers to make money by buying into pyramid-type marketing platforms. The many ways you can be scammed are endless. Keep it simple and ignore them all.

- If you are planning a move, supply the post office with the appropriate change of address information. This ensures your mail doesn't go astray and land in the hands of criminals who know how to use that information to assume your identity—or to provide it to someone else for that same purpose.

The Canadian Marketing Association (CMA), a national private trade organization that advocates responsible marketing practices, advises Canadians who would like to reduce their unwanted advertising mail to consider registering with that organization's Do Not Contact Service. This is a free online service that removes the names of individuals from marketing mail lists. By adding your name to this list, you will reduce the amount of unsolicited mail you receive, but not eliminate it completely. The service only removes your name from member businesses. You will still need to be vigilant in managing your mail and restricting the requests you choose to respond to.

Chapter Seven

Have I Got a Deal for You!

~

THE VOICE OF TELEPHONE FRAUD

I t's endlessly annoying, and if the number of times I disconnect from a telemarketer are any indication of what the rest of Canadians have to deal with, it's extremely surprising that businesses continue to use this method of communication to try to sell their goods. But despite consumers constantly complaining that yet another supper hour has been disrupted by a salesperson, someone has to be buying what these people are selling. Go online and Google "telemarketing in Canada" and you'll find several companies that provide telemarketing services to businesses, and others who sell telemarketing lists of names and contact numbers. Still other businesses geared to the telemarketing industry, Infogroup for example, outline the best way for companies to build their own telemarketing and direct mail lists to get the most out of targeting the more than 12 million consumers in this country. And according to one CBC News story, as recently as 2006, Canadian businesses spent $4.1 billion on telemarketing in this country, "generating $26.1 billion in sales and creating 155,000 jobs."

At the same time, crooked telephone schemes designed to trick the public into buying something of little or no value at an inflated price, signing on for services they don't need or getting them to provide personal details that could be used to undermine an individual's financial or personal stability have been around as long as telemarketers—longer if you consider the deceitful peddlers of the past who promoted moonshine as a magic medicine and dusting powder as a cure for lice. TD Canada Trust's fraud department estimates that "telemarketing fraud costs Canadians more than $100 million every year."

In order to protect Canadians, the Canadian Radio-television and Telecommunications Commission (CRTC) regulates telemarketing. Companies must follow certain rules or be liable for considerable fines.

Generally speaking, it's perfectly legal for a business to use telephone solicitation as part of its marketing strategy, but the calls must come through between 9:00 AM and 9:30 PM on weekdays, and between 10:00 AM and 6:00 PM on Saturday and Sunday in any given time zone. Telemarketers can also dial randomly, which means they can actually connect with unlisted numbers. Also, legitimate telemarketers have to identify themselves, state the name of the organization they are representing and outline the purpose of the call. They must also, on request, connect an individual with an employee, manager or other delegate from the company they are representing.

The dos and don'ts of telemarketing are considerable, and the consistent hang-ups must be discouraging to employees in the industry. But when you take into account the low overhead, it's understandable why many organizations continue to use telemarketers.

But how do you know if the call disrupting your family gathering is legitimate or not?

How can you learn to identify the voice of telephone fraud?

MAY I SPEAK WITH…

When "CB" (name withheld to protect her identity) answered the phone at work one spring day in 2012 and the gentleman on the other end asked for her by name, it seemed like an ordinary request. Her friends and family all knew where she worked, as did her credit card company, doctor's office, hairdresser, Revenue Canada and many other official contacts.

CB is an affable sort of woman, and so the conversation flowed quite naturally between CB and the male caller. At least it seemed to flow until what CB calls "red flags" went up.

"He said he was entering my name in the Publishers Clearing House draw for $25,000—sounded good," she said. "But he needed to know my preferred credit card. That's when I hung up. I figured if he needed to know my credit card, there was something fishy going on there—I'm not giving that information out."

CB also thought it was odd that the caller was going to enter her name in a Publishers Clearing House draw when she didn't subscribe to any magazines. Where would he have gotten her name?

She was thankful that she hadn't divulged anything that could have compromised her safety. And although it was a disturbing experience, she didn't give it a second thought.

Then less than a week later, a woman phoned and said she was going to enter CB's name for a $500 draw. The female caller didn't say who was having the draw, only that CB could "make $500 just by standing there talking to her while I was working."

Again, CB hung up on the caller. "I didn't think anyone honest would be doing that," she said. "I'm very skeptical—cautious."

A few days after that call, CB received yet another call at work. The male caller asked for her by name. "I think it was the same man," CB said. "I didn't give him a chance to say anything— I just cut him off. But I asked him how he got my name and he said off the Internet, and hung up."

CB found it strange that the man hung up after answering her question. Why, she wondered, would he hang up when she couldn't identify him? When she dialled *69, the number came up as "Blocked."

Who was this individual or organization calling her, and why did they persist? Even more disturbing were two obvious questions: how did he know where she worked and why had none of her workmates received a call when she wasn't around? The calls only arrived when CB was at work, which made her feel like she was being specifically targeted and harassed, for whatever reason. Maybe someone was following her and watching what she was doing? "I just think it was really strange," she said.

By this point, CB was duly spooked. After talking with her employer about the phone calls she had received, she called the RCMP, who advised her to call the Canadian Anti-Fraud Centre. Unfortunately, the caller ID at her workplace only registered

"Unknown Caller," so without a telephone number, the police and the CAFC couldn't do much, which didn't ease CB's concern. It was additionally disconcerting that neither the CAFC nor the RCMP could provide a reasonable explanation on how the caller knew where CB worked.

The only safeguard CB could administer was to inform her co-workers about the strange phone calls. "If anyone calls asking for me again, tell them I no longer work here," she told them.

As of the writing of this book, CB hasn't learned the identity of the man or the woman who had called her, nor did she discover how they knew where she worked. CB didn't give the callers any information that could have compromised her finances or led to the theft of her identity. But the experience left her feeling vulnerable, like she was a target in someone's list of intended victims and it was only a matter of time before they collected the information they were looking for.

Even if CB doesn't receive another phone call, her life has been altered by the experience. While not prone to paranoia, CB is doubly cautions about everything she does. And she always wonders if the man who called her workplace will call again—when she's at work.

SERVICE SCAMS ABOUND

There are almost as many telephone scams circulating as there are email scams. Callers promoting an offer of low interest rates on mortgages or credit cards are one example of what the CAFC calls a "service scam." Sometimes the offer is delivered by an individual or at other times you hear a recorded announcement when you answer the phone. In any case, these interruptions to our lives are annoying and can be potentially damaging.

A service scam is typically defined as "any false, deceptive or misleading promotion of services or solicitation for services" that often include "offers for telecommunications, internet, finance, medical and energy services" as well as "extended warranties, insurance and sales service." Notice that the "services" being offered are what most of us would consider among life's necessities—we all need medical care, electricity, insurance and so on. So when a scammer calls about one of these services, it's not uncommon that for every dozen or so telephone calls the individual makes, he or she might hit on someone who's interested in the "service."

As with any other scam, these service scams evolve with the times and frequently piggyback on a recent news concern or a legitimate product or service that's introduced to the marketplace.

The "Hydro Power Saver" is one example of a service scam. In February 2012, RCMP in Weyburn, Saskatchewan, warned residents in that area about a telephone solicitor claiming to represent a "local or provincial hydro company" and allegedly offering for sale the "Hydro Power Saver," which, if installed, could save them as much as 50 percent on their power bills. The caller explained that the device was simple to use. All consumers needed to do was plug it into the wall and voila, like magic, it would stabilize "voltages and reduce currents on power supplies or appliances of a consumer's household," thereby improving overall efficiency.

An article in the *Weyburn Review* explained how, once hooked on what sounds like a great idea, the consumer is "connected" with a supervisor. At that point the caller asks for a credit card number and address or requests a cheque or money order for amounts ranging from $130 to $189 and says to expect a "Hydro Power Saver" in the mail. In some cases a product is delivered, but it does not have any Canadian Safety Standards markings, is priced beyond its value and doesn't do what the solicitor claimed it would do, namely reduce the consumer's power bill. Other cases of bogus solicitation involve similar requests for money from the victim, but a product is never delivered.

While telephone solicitation might have been a valid method of marketing a product in the past, with the number of scams now circulating, the best advice you can heed is to avoid doing business with anyone by phone, especially when you haven't initiated the contact.

THE LUCKY WINNER RECEIVES...

Another common telephone scam is what the CAFC calls the "prize pitch." The prize pitch has been around for a long time, and it circulates in all forms of communication: land mail, email and telephone. In this scenario, a telephone scammer calls to tell you that you've won a prize, which could be anything from a "coin collection" to a cruise for two. Of course, conditions are usually tied to the receipt of these "prizes." For example, the intended victim might be asked to supply a credit card number or other financial information.

I remember being targeted by this scam. I'd apparently won a wonderful Caribbean cruise. All I had to do was provide the caller with a credit card number to cover the $350 service fee. At the time, almost any kind of fraudulent practice was foreign to me. My naïveté was exactly what these con artists were looking for—an innocent, trusting, working-class person who'd love a holiday and wouldn't think it outrageous to pay a nominal service fee. I'm also softhearted by nature. I remember thinking how hard it must be for the caller to make a living as a telemarketer, how she must have a husband and kids at home and was trying to add to the family coffers by picking up part-time work as a telephone solicitor. The least I could do was hear her out and maintain a cordial manner in the process.

Of course, I am also a journalist. So although the prospect of jet-setting somewhere warm in the middle of a cold Alberta winter excited me, I have a suspicious nature. I started asking questions that resulted in answers that only led to more questions; the caller's answers didn't make any sense to me. And when the woman started barking her replies and questioning my right to even ask these questions, I hung up. Fortunately, I hadn't given her my credit card number.

Creativity is a prerequisite for con artists of all stripes, and telephone scammers are no exception. Given the right audience, these criminals use sound psychology to issue their plea, making everything sound so reasonable and inevitably coercing their way into a victim's pocketbook. And to offer proof of their legitimacy, sweepstakes scammers have been known to set up bogus web sites and give their victims "pass codes" to check in and reassure themselves that everything is valid and legal.

News Alert:
Woman Loses Big in Sweepstakes Scam

Another scam commonly perpetrated through the telephone is the "sweepstakes scam." The small, unincorporated community of Taghum is a picturesque hamlet located on the southeastern tip of British Columbia's Kootenay region. Visitors to the area are treated to tree-lined hillsides sweeping the horizon, lush vegetation and crisp, clean air. The beauty of the place never grows old for residents. Here, in this corner of the world, life is full of wonder and stands in stark contrast to the rush and frenzy of a busy city.

This kind of innocuous lifestyle in a small town can lend itself to producing a type of naïveté in its residents. When immersed in such a wholesome environment, it's hard to imagine the sometimes-harsh realities the world can dish out.

Perhaps it was this innocence that made Alice (name changed to protect her privacy) vulnerable to the wiles of a heartless criminal when the elderly woman received a telephone call in August 2011. The caller, allegedly living in Jamaica at the time, told Alice that she'd just snagged a $5.5 million win in the "Winner's Circle International" contest.

Now, for the more jaded among us, red flags would have immediately gone up. However, Alice was excited and not immediately

HAVE I GOT A DEAL FOR YOU!

183

suspicious. She remembered entering a magazine contest a while before; the caller must have been referring to that contest.

The caller went on to explain what was involved in Alice collecting her winnings, beginning with the requirement that she send $25,000 in advance to cover any taxes incurred by the windfall—$5.5 million was a lot of money, hence the steep taxation fee, the caller must have explained.

Making this payment was a considerably complicated process, however. A quickly befuddled Alice was given instructions to send some of the money via Western Union, some directly to individuals at various destinations in Jamaica and some through bank transfers.

According to the *Arrow Lakes News* in Nakusp, BC, Alice was instructed "not to discuss the winnings (and tax exemption) with anyone, even family members, until [she] received the jackpot."

Alice couldn't believe her good fortune. She could help so many family members and friends with such a large amount of money. After carrying out the caller's instructions, all Alice had to do was wait until the required payments were received and she could share her good news.

But when a second call, allegedly from "Winner's Circle International," came through asking Alice for more money, she started to get a little nervous. She was uncertain of what steps she should take at that point, but she reasoned that she had already sent $25,000, and if she wanted to recoup the money she had sent, she needed to continue to comply with the caller's requests.

This story does not end well. Alice lost $78,000 before she finally contacted the authorities. Defrauded of her life savings, Alice is one of many vulnerable seniors who've been targeted by telephone scam artists like this one. Sadly, because many of these operations are based in other countries, the authorities usually can't do much to retrieve the money lost or to discover and prosecute the offenders.

The elderly are particularly vulnerable to these ploys for several reasons. First and foremost, it's not completely out of the realm of possibility that they may have won a prize when, as Alice did (see News Alert), they had indeed entered a contest. After all, we've heard news stories about people winning sweepstakes before. And TV documentaries have shown film crews filming as an announcer walks up the front steps of an ordinary American household, giant cheque and microphone in hand, and knocks on the door, waiting for the winner to answer in anticipation of changing their life forever. Someone has to win, right?

Another factor making the elderly vulnerable to this sweepstakes ploy is their heartfelt desire to do something nice for their family. They've lived a life full of challenges and would find it comforting to know they can relieve some of the financial burden off the shoulders of their loved ones. The elderly often live alone and don't have someone around to overhear a conversation like the one Alice experienced and to provide another opinion on its legitimacy. That isolation usually works in favour of the fraudster.

As well, the "contest officials" making the telephone calls are well versed on the techniques they need to use to confuse their victims. The longer they can keep someone on the telephone, the closer they are to closing the deal. Once a victim has completed the instructions and sent the money requested, that victim feels obligated to continue with any further requests to ensure they receive their winnings. And if they do become suspicious, the victims are often reluctant to report their experience to the authorities because they're embarrassed to acknowledge the possibility they've fallen for a scam. This is one reason why the actual number of victims of fraud and identity theft is unknown, and many times is greater than the statistics portray.

A PLEA FOR HELP

It's six o'clock on a snowy, winter evening. The dinner dishes have been washed and put away, and a warm slice of lemon loaf sits on the coffee table, waiting as an elderly woman carries her freshly steeped cup of tea into the living room and turns on the TV to watch the evening news.

Glancing outside her living room window, the woman is grateful for the comfort and safety of her home. It looks wicked outside. Stories about the icy roads and poor visibility don't wait for the weather announcer—they're prime time news tonight. Motorists are being warned to stay off the roads if at all possible. The woman shudders to think anyone she knows might be out there.

The ring of the telephone interrupts her thoughts.

"Hello," the woman answers.

"Hi, Gran," a muffled voice utters. The telephone reception is poor, and it sounds like the man at the other end of the line is standing out in that inclement weather talking on a cellphone.

"Jason?" the woman says, immediately anxious that her 19-year-old grandson is out in the storm. "Is that you, Jason?"

"Yes, Gran," the voice continues. "I'm in trouble...I need your help."

From what the woman could make out of the fractured conversation, which seemed to cut out several times before she could gather the entire story, her youngest grandson had been driving his mother's car when he hit a patch of black ice and fishtailed several times before sailing into a ditch and smashing into a culvert. He said his mother loaned him the car because he was going out of town for a few days, and he needed new tires on his own car before he drove it any distance in this weather.

"Mom's car is in bad shape," the man explained. "But the tow truck driver said the company he works for could fix it up in a day or two and Mom would never know it had been in an accident."

When the woman asks about insurance covering the cost, the man says he didn't want to go that route. Calling his insurance company would increase his rates, and because of his young age, those rates were high already, he explained.

"Please, Gram," he pleads, asking if she could give him a loan.

By the end of the phone conversation, the woman has agreed to send money to fix the car and to cover a hotel room for her grandson for the next couple of nights; like most grandmas, she has a hard time saying no to her grandson. And after a heated debate between the woman and her grandson, she also agreed to keep the incident to herself—Jason would never get the keys to the family car again if his mother knew of the accident.

While the above example is fictitious, it depicts a scenario that unfortunately hits all too many seniors across Canada. It's known by law enforcement as the "emergency" or "grandparent" scam. In March 2012, CBC News aired a story about one 87-year-old woman (she asked not to be identified because she was embarrassed by the incident) who not only emptied her bank account but also took out a $5000 line of credit from her bank to help a man she believed was her grandson. This woman lost a total of $20,000 before her son discovered the fraud.

The CAFC received 1537 complaints from residents receiving emergency/grandparent scam phone calls between January and May 2011; 143 of those individuals followed through on the requests for money and lost a total of $873,537.31. While some individuals, like the woman above, eventually come forward with the aid of family or friends who connect them with the authorities, they are the minority. Embarrassment prevents what sources estimate is an astounding 95 percent of victims from reporting the incident.

1-900 SCAMS

This scam incorporates a combination of land mail and telephone fraud, which can easily add confusion to the mix when it comes to assessing if what you've just pulled out of your mailbox is on the up-and-up or not.

The scam starts off with a letter in the mail that states you've won money, but in order to find out how much you'll receive, you need to call a 1-900 number—for security reasons, of course. Recipients of these notices are informed that there is a charge per minute and are given the average duration of each call, making them sound honest. However, when you make that call, you are connected with a computerized voice recording, which extends the call considerably longer than the aforementioned average length of one minute. At the end of the journey, it's not uncommon for individuals to find out they've won only a loonie or two. Compare that to the average $35 per phone call charged to your phone bill and it's easy to see that once again, you've been exposed to a scam.

IDENTIFYING THE LEGITIMATE CALL

Like everyone else in Canada, I seem to be inundated with calls from telephone marketers flogging everything from low interest rates for any debt I might be carrying to a cruise I've won a few dozen times by now. So when, during one supper hour, I received an odd call from a man who said he was a representative of the bank I deal with, I was leery. After all, I had received a lot of email spam allegedly from banking institutions asking me to follow up on some emergency or another.

Because the gentleman asked for me by name, I gave him a moment of my time. He went on to explain that a selection of compact discs with banking information had gone missing in transport between two locations—exactly why this information was transported by disc still eludes me, but that's another matter. At that point I was mortified to learn that the discs contained personal details of each bank client, including account numbers, investment details, Social Insurance Numbers, birthdates, addresses—everything. The man said the bank was informing their clients of the incident.

Now, I don't know how you might have felt, but my cautious skepticism about the legitimacy of this telephone call went into overdrive.

"How do I know you're from the bank?" I asked, waiting for him to ask me for my account number or some other bit of information that would verify he was actually a fraudster looking for easy access to my accounts—and my life.

But he didn't ask me those questions.

Instead, the caller said he understood my concern and invited me to call a toll-free telephone number to confirm what he was telling me. I thanked him and immediately hung up the telephone. Then, because it was the end of the business day and I could no longer get in touch with my personal banker, I dialled my usual telephone banking number instead of using the toll-free number he gave me—he may not have asked for specific personal information but I still didn't trust him. In fact, I believed I was on to some form of con game and I was anxious to alert my bank about it.

Once I bypassed the automated system and connected with an individual, I shared my story. Imagine my shock when I discovered it was indeed true! Two CDs had gone missing. What's more, the banking representative explained that this type of loss happens quite frequently, but customers are only informed of the missing information when it can't be tracked down.

"I wouldn't worry," explained the representative. "The Office of the Privacy Commissioner has been notified of the loss, as well as details on the information contained in the CDs."

The Office of the Privacy Commissioner (OPC) of Canada is responsible for advocating for our privacy rights. According to the official website, their responsibilities include:

- *Investigating complaints, conducting audits and pursuing court action under two federal laws*

- *Publicly reporting on the personal information-handling practices of public and private sector organizations*

- *Supporting, undertaking and publishing research into privacy issues*

- *Promoting public awareness and understanding of privacy issues*

I expect the banking representative I spoke with shared the information about OPC to provide me with some sort of peace of mind. Although I was still distressed, it eased my concerns somewhat knowing my bank voluntarily disclosed the privacy breach—something organizations are encouraged but not legally mandated to do in Canada.

Once a privacy breach, or "incident" as the OPC refers to it, is reported, a file is opened and the breach is monitored. In a nutshell, the OPC wants to know details about what happened, how it happened, if the individuals affected—in this case the bank's clients whose information appeared on the missing discs—have been notified, and what measures are being instituted to ensure this particular kind of breach doesn't happen again.

Still, there was the question about my private information. I couldn't just change my name and move because of the incident, and I felt somewhat exposed realizing that my personal information could have been distributed to criminals looking for new identity-theft victims. I could change account numbers and close old credit cards and open new ones, which would provide some measure of comfort. But no matter what I did, my personal information was out there, and I was more vulnerable now than I had ever been before.

While a firm solution hasn't been forthcoming in the missing CD story, it is a good example of how to handle calls of this nature. When someone calls identifying themselves as a representative of a financial institution you deal with, you should question their motives. However, under no circumstances should you give out any information. If they present you with a telephone number to follow up on the issue they're addressing, use only the numbers you know. It might take a while before you're directed to the appropriate department, but you'll have the assurance that you know the person you're dealing with.

This next example comes from the pages of Graham McWaters and Gary Ford's book *The Canadian Guide to Protecting Yourself from Identity Theft and Other Fraud.* I use this example because the caller in this case sounds legitimate, and the issue he addresses is a serious one. Unlike my experience, where I was immediately suspicious, the victim in this case was willing to accept the caller at face value. In this scenario, an individual received a call that allegedly originated from MasterCard's security department. The caller identified himself by giving his badge number and informed the man that MasterCard believed his card had been compromised: a $397.99 charge for an "anti-telemarketing device" from a company in California had been added.

When the individual denied making the charge, the caller explained that MasterCard had been "watching this company for a while now, especially for charges ranging from $249 to $499, just under the $500 purchase pattern that flags most cards."

Although disturbing, the caller's story sounded plausible.

The caller then gave the individual instructions on how to follow up on the alleged scam, instructing him to call the 1-800 number on the back of his card. In addition, the caller assigned the individual with a case number. So when the caller asked for the man's three-digit security number, found at the end of most MasterCard account numbers, the individual gave it without hesitation. After all, the caller *did not* ask for his credit card number—only the three-digit security number. What harm could it do?

As you might guess, this scenario did not end well. When the man received his next MasterCard statement in the mail, he noticed several charges he did not make. Reflecting back to the call he'd received earlier that month, it became clear—he'd been scammed. How the caller had managed to get the man's 16-digit credit card number remained a mystery, but once he acquired the three-digit security number, he was off shopping.

Again, the main warning here is to keep your private information private at all times. If the call you receive is legitimate, no one will pressure you for any information. If you feel compelled to follow up on the phone call, use the contact numbers you have, not the ones given to you by the caller. While the extra steps might take a bit of time, they'll protect you in the long run.

CELLPHONE POPULARITY POSES NEW OPPORTUNITY

Just because you might not have a landline doesn't mean you won't receive scam calls on your cellphone. The same techniques criminals use to defraud you of your hard-earned cash on your home telephone can be used to con you on your cellphone. In fact, it could be far more destructive to you financially if you pay for ringtones you didn't order or sign up for some other service you can't later disconnect.

The Australian Competition and Consumer Commission explains that one reason why cellphone scams are particularly dangerous is because they can rack up expensive phone bills when victims redial the phone number attributed to a missed call. That's because your return telephone call could have been "redirected to a premium rate service [in Canada and the U.S. it is frequently a 1-900 number] without your knowledge, which means you will be charged a lot of money for every minute you're kept on the line." If the victim ends up subscribing to what he's led to believe is a free ringtone or is talked into accepting any other "prize," it could cost more money. In addition, some of these services can't be easily cancelled, which means the charges attributed to that service are also ongoing. Similarly, responding to unknown text messages could also cost cellphone customers high user fees.

The best advice when it comes to dealing with unwanted calls and texts is to ignore them. If you don't recognize a phone number on your call display, do not call back. If the call is legitimate, the individual will leave a message or will call you back later. The same holds true for any texts you receive from unknown numbers. Simply delete the text.

TELEPHONE FRAUD SAFETY CHECKLIST

- When receiving an unsolicited phone call from someone offering to sell you a product or provide a service, check your call display. The CRTC requires telemarketers to "display the originating calling number or an alternate number where the call originator can be reached." The exception to this is when the number can't be displayed for some kind of technical reason, but if so, I'd rather be safe than sorry and would hang up immediately.

- If the product or service the telemarketer is selling interests you, take your time before making a purchase. A legitimate company will give you the time you need to verify their existence and find out more objective information on the product before you buy.

- If you do engage in conversation with the caller, never provide any financial information. That includes credit card numbers, expiry dates and security numbers and even your home address and email address. Do your homework first, and have the company and product validated before finalizing a transaction.

- Never send cash! TD Canada Trust warns that "criminal telemarketers often ask you to send cash or a money order, rather than provide a cheque or credit card number." This only makes sense— many criminals can't process a credit card transaction.

- Keep detailed notes of any telemarketing purchase you make, including the caller's name and identification number; the name, address and telephone number of the company they represent; and the product, cost, method of payment and promised delivery date.

- If you receive a call from someone telling you that you've won a prize or hit it big in some new sweepstakes or contest, hang up. As tempting as it might be, the chances of this being a real claim are highly improbable at best. And if it is the real deal, the company issuing the prize or money will find another way to make contact with you.

- Never provide personal information over the phone, and never trust someone you don't know. This warning should be common sense and may sound redundant—it has appeared several times in this book—but it's a caution that can't be stressed enough, especially when faced with something out of the ordinary, or something that sounds remarkably plausible.

- If you receive any variation of the "emergency phone call," be wary. The majority of the time this will be a scam. However, to ease your concern, pepper your caller with questions to validate their identity—their full name, for example, or the name of their pet or the make and model of their vehicle. In addition, tell them you will call them back and check for yourself if that individual is in trouble.

- Use the Internet to verify any company trying to contact you by phone. Check their website and whether they're a member of the Better Business Bureau.

- If you are concerned that a caller has compromised your personal information, file a report with the Canadian Anti-Fraud Centre as soon as possible.

- Be wary of any caller telling you that they are offering you a chance to get in on a special promotion that is expiring that day. This is a scam—hang up immediately.

- Be wary of callers offering to demonstrate a product at your home. Again, this is most likely a scam and it's best to terminate the phone call.

- If you're concerned about becoming a victim of 1-900 scams, some telephone companies will block 900 and 976 numbers at no charge to their customers. Other companies charge a nominal fee for the same service.

- If an unknown caller addresses you by your name or asks specific questions about your household, hang up. Criminals looking for break-and-enter opportunities will sometimes call a home to find out how many people live at the residence and the times of day when the home is vacant.

- And finally, if you've had it with telephone marketers, consider registering your telephone numbers with the Do Not Call Registry, a service offered by the federal government. You can do this online at www.lnnte-dncl.gc.ca/nrt-ntr-eng or by calling 1-866-580-DNCL (3625). Be aware that it takes 31 days for the number you register to be added to the DNC list, and political organizations or candidates, registered charities, opinion polling firms, market researchers collecting information or conducting surveys (but not trying to make a sale) and newspapers are exempt from adhering to this list. Note also that any organization you've previously done business with can still contact you, and your registration with the program has an expiry date, which you will receive on registration. That means if you want to continue to be on the list, you will need to re-register at that time.

~

Chapter Eight

The Ugly Truth About Mortgage Fraud

~

PULLING THE RUG OUT FROM UNDER YOU

Imagine this…

You've worked hard all your life, played the tortoise and slowly but steadily chipped away at your mortgage until finally you can burn the loan papers and celebrate complete and total ownership of your home. You no longer share that privilege with the bank; it's all yours, free and clear.

By this point in your life you're probably considering retirement, but you decide to plug away for a few more years to flesh out your savings. You'd like to travel, maybe plan some adventurous excursion to see the polar bears in Churchill or some other extravagance you simply couldn't afford before.

And then the day you retire arrives! You can breathe! Sure, monthly bills still have to be paid, but the bulk of your life's work has ensured you have a roof over your head and money in the bank to buy a few extras.

That's what septuagenarian Norman Gettel thought. The Richmond, BC, resident left his career as a printer in the late 1990s, and he was enjoying the retired life. Gettel didn't accomplish all he did without working hard, and that same due diligence ensured he maintained a comfortable retirement. So when his annual property assessment outlining the taxes he owed didn't arrive in the spring of 2008, Gettel addressed the problem immediately, telephoning the BC Assessment Authority to let them know of the situation.

He was stunned when he was told that he didn't receive the assessment because he no longer owned the property.

Gettel personally went to the Land Titles Office, arguing that he did not sell his home, only to discover the property documents they had on file said quite the opposite. According to those documents, Gettel had sold his home, valued at the time at more than $600,000, in July 2007. What was worse still was that the individual who allegedly purchased his home had immediately proceeded to take out a $400,000 mortgage on it with CIBC but had yet to make even one of the $2600 monthly mortgage payments on the property.

While Gettel's story is shocking, it is not unique.

Gettel had experienced a case of mortgage fraud, a crime that is becoming increasingly prevalent. In 2011 alone, Equifax Canada reported an astounding $400 million worth of mortgage fraud in this country—and that number only represents the cases they are aware of.

"Mortgages are the biggest bang for the buck," John Russo, vice-president and legal counsel for Equifax Canada Inc. said in a press release. "So when credit gets tougher to get, that leads to more people falsifying documents, giving false pay stubs, inflating their income, kind of fudging things to get a home."

In Gettel's case, the fudging that went on to "sell" and re-mortgage his home came in the form of a stranger who impersonated Gettel using a BC driver's licence and provincial health care card. A *Vancouver Sun* story explained that someone unknown to the senior simply waltzed into a Surrey law office, claimed to be Gettel and signed over his property for "$1.00 And Natural Love And Affection."

According to the documents, the "buyer" was an "Oleg Balan," and when Gettel finally learned of the fraud, the bank providing the $400,000 mortgage was getting ready to "enforce its security" on the property.

As the investigation into Gettel's nightmare unfolded, it appeared to have been perpetrated by an individual who'd attempted and was occasionally successful at conducting similar ruses in other parts of the Greater Vancouver Area. In Gettel's case, it took more than six months and $10,000 in legal fees before the rightful title to his home was restored to him.

The outstanding mortgage, on the other hand, was another story—that was something the Land Title Office and CIBC had to address.

Why Commit Mortgage Fraud?

The Canadian Mortgage and Housing Corporation (CMHC) states mortgage fraud occurs when "someone deliberately misrepresents information on a loan application, to obtain mortgage financing that likely would not have approved if the truth had been known." The Criminal Intelligence Services Canada (CISC) explains that while the reasons for mortgage fraud can be quite diverse, they typically fall into three main categories: to enable the commission of other criminal activities; for profit; and for shelter.

Although details weren't known about whether the individual committing the fraud in Gettel's case worked alone or was part of a criminal conglomerate, the motive for the crime was clearly money. Another story coming out of Alberta in 2010 demonstrates just how financially lucrative mortgage fraud can be. A mass operation of 14 interconnected groups worked together to pull off an estimated $140 million in illegally acquired profits.

CBC News broke the story in May of that year after the Bank of Montréal announced it was suing "hundreds of people in Alberta, including lawyers, mortgage brokers and four of its own employees." The announcement came after an investigation in 2006 into what banking representatives called "irregularities," discovered a complex scam that threatened to cost the bank as much as $30 million, according to some reports. Although investigators suspected other financial institutions were also victims of this scheme, the Bank of Montréal made their involvement public in the hope of recouping some of their losses, as well as to send a "strong message" to fraudsters that the bank will not tolerate fraud and "will pursue [it] very aggressively."

The CBC story explained how the "ringleaders" in the multi-million-dollar operation would "identify the worst house in a good neighbourhood" and purchase it at fair market value, often using a "straw buyer," the term given to an individual who is making a purchase for another person who wouldn't otherwise be able to make that purchase. This isn't illegal—unless, as CISC explains, the straw buyer "is an individual who pretends to be a legitimate buyer for a property but in reality is in collusion with another criminally inclined individual to further a mortgage scam."

In the Alberta case, select individuals were approached, including new immigrants. These people allowed their names to be used to obtain the mortgage on a home. Often, a fictitious job and wage was provided to the straw buyer, making him appear to have the means to make the mortgage payments. For their trouble, these straw buyers were promised as much as $8000.

The ringleaders would then "convince the bank [the house] was worth much more because of the neighbourhood it was in." In this way, the bank would provide an "inflated mortgage, and the ringleaders would pocket the difference." Not only would the straw buyer never see a penny of the money he was promised, but he was also left on the hook for the mortgage with no real ability to pay for it.

Seventeen lawyers were among the individuals named in the bank's lawsuit for allegedly assisting in creating the necessary legal documents to pull off this massive scheme. Several mortgage brokers along with four banking representatives were also named in the suit, which is still before the courts.

There are other reasons aside from an immediate financial reward that a straw buyer would be used to further an illegal venture. A buyer anxious to hide his assets from the government for taxation purposes is one reason. Another is when a home is needed for marijuana grow-ops or meth labs. In any case, allowing your name to stand as a straw buyer is never a good idea.

Financial profit is often as powerful a motivator to ordinary folk as it is to organized crime. Many cases of mortgage fraud involve family members, leaving the innocent victim distraught over the loss of a relationship as well as the monetary loss.

The Dunford story (see News Alert) shows that someone you love can commit mortgage fraud without your knowledge. It can leave you in financial and emotional ruin, and all too often the perpetrator of the crime receives little to no legal ramifications.

Other forms of mortgage fraud are disguised as a helping hand out of a difficult situation. We've all struggled financially at one time or another, and there may have been times when some of us couldn't make our mortgage payments. If you've ever been in that situation, you might understand the temptation to take someone up on an offer to purchase your home at a reduced rate or provide you with a low-interest-rate loan. The problem is that not everyone offering to help is genuine; far too frequently that help is presented by a con artist whose only interest is to pad their own pockets at your expense.

News Alert:
Woman Defrauded by Sister

The Labour Day long weekend in 2006 didn't go off as planned for Peterborough residents Sharon and Trevor Dunford. What was going to be a restful weekend in Niagara Falls evolved into the beginnings of a legal dispute that took years to iron out.

The story, which made headlines in several Toronto-area newspapers, began when the Dunfords made a surprise visit to the home in St. Catharines that Sharon co-owned with her estranged sister, referred to as Victoria Van A, on the couple's way out of town. Sharon and her sister came to own the house after their mother died in 2000 and bequeathed it to the sisters equally. The will also stipulated that Victoria could live in the home, provided she maintain it and pay for the utilities.

The visit was certainly a surprise, but quite a different one than Sharon expected. When she arrived at the house, it was empty. The interior of the home was badly damaged and smelled of smoke, and the yard was in disarray. Worse still, neighbours told Sharon that the house had just sold, and her sister was nowhere to be found.

Impossible, the Dunfords told *Sun* reporters later on. "We knew she couldn't have sold the house because Sharon owns half of it," Trevor said.

Unfortunately for Sharon, the house had indeed been sold. Although Sharon never signed the required paperwork, another woman impersonating Sharon had forged her signature. According to one news article, Victoria, the woman posing as Sharon and the buyer all used the same lawyer, and that lawyer neglected to thoroughly check the woman's identification.

Luckily for Sharon, she and her husband discovered the fraudulent sale of the sisters' family home within a 21-day grace period established under the Land Titles Act in St. Catharines for the notification of any errors or omissions before the final certification of the sale documents. Real-estate lawyer Adam Baker told reporters that had the deed been registered in Peterborough, the Dunfords might have been too late to do anything because deeds are processed more quickly in that community.

Thanks to the quick action of all involved, Sharon regained her half-ownership of the home. However, her battle was far from over. Victoria had left with her share of the house, and Sharon now faced a co-ownership with someone she didn't know and a home that was rundown considerably from its earlier glory. Plus, she had to pay $9000 in back taxes, not to mention the extensive legal fees she incurred in the process.

In February 2007, fraud charges were laid against Victoria and her female accomplice, along with charges of personation and forgery. Later that same year, the charges were dropped when a judge determined the case would be better served in a civil court. The Dunfords didn't have the means to pay for the court battle—the lengthy legal struggle had already depleted all their resources and maxed out their credit options. In January 2008 the Dunfords learned that some of their legal fees would be reimbursed through the Land Titles Assurance Fund, which was established to help people embroiled in disputes over property titles.

This type of mortgage scam is a variation of the old con standby: the bait and switch. Once an offer is made, and the desperate homeowner accepts the offer, an assortment of complicated documents is presented, signatures are penned and the deed done—or undone, in this case. What the homeowner doesn't realize is that in this last-ditch attempt to maintain the residence, he very well may have signed a quitclaim deed (a document removing the owner from any rights or title to the property) or inadvertently transferred the property interest to the con artist's name.

Another scam anxious homeowners struggling financially should be aware of is when someone offers to bail them out of their debt by purchasing the home for a price that mirrors the remaining mortgage on that home. The con artist then allows the original owners to live in the home, paying rent of course. And of course, the rent is higher than the original mortgage would have been, which means the renter is now in worse shape. Eventually, the renter once again can't make the payments and ends up losing everything. Evicted, these individuals end up homeless and lose whatever equity they might have had in the first place.

I HAVE THIS PIECE OF LAND FOR SALE

We've all heard the old line often delivered to gullible and naïve individuals: "And if you believe that, I've got some swampland in Florida for sale." Some sources suggest this saying stemmed from a confidence trick—a fraud committed once the con artist gains a victim's trust and confidence. The confidence trick originated in the early 20th century when con men would offer to sell deeds on landmarks such as the Statue of Liberty or some other property they didn't own. It's an old scam that remains lucrative to this day, probably because it's difficult to believe someone has the audacity to try to pull something like that off; people generally believe you when you say you have something to sell.

The village of Granisle is a pretty little community tucked away in the rolling mountains of northern British Columbia and nestled along the shores of the province's longest lake, the 180-kilometre-long Babine Lake. Granisle was once considerably larger than it is today, with as many as 3000 residents making their livelihood from the nearby copper mines. But copper isn't a renewable resource, and once the veins dried up so did the town. Houses stood vacant.

Nice homes on the market for $20,000 couldn't sell—you couldn't give them away. And business at the local motel dwindled to a slow crawl.

All was not lost, however. Instead of looking at the glass half-empty, Granisle hoped it could tempt visitors north off the much nicer Highway 16 and along the 49 winding and bumpy roads of Highway 118. The area is rich with vegetation, teeming with wild-life, a playground for outdoor adventure enthusiasts and a haven from the busyness of life. It was a perfect resort destination.

Richard Bryan Minard (aka Bryan Allen Richards) could certainly see the village's potential. So much so that the American-born, self-proclaimed preacher and Christian rock-jock honed in on the area with an idea that he would have no problems selling. Minard, who went by the name of Bryan Richards during his short residence in the neighbouring Bulkley Valley, decided that it would be lucrative to sell timeshares to a resort he and a partner were alleg-edly developing from pre-existing structures in the community.

Granisle Time Share Condos was a huge draw to the Ameri-can hunters that Minard was targeting. And you couldn't blame the sportsmen for their interest. For a reasonable $5000 to $10,000, interested clients were guaranteed a two-week stay every year for the rest of their lives.

It was a nominal fee for vacationing at a pristine location with endless opportunities for hunting, fishing, bird watching, hik-ing, photography and so much more. Yes, Minard could potentially turn this former copper town into a gold mine.

The problem was, Minard didn't own the condos he was trying to sell! He could just as well have been selling swampland in Florida—he was taking money from people without having a product. And he pedalled his scam for quite some time before suspicions were raised and enough evidence against him was collected to warrant the RCMP taking Minard in for questioning. That's when the authorities discovered Minard had been using an assumed name, and that his time in Canada only added to the long list of charges he was wanted for south of the border. Minard ended up facing the authorities in an American courthouse after being returned to his home country.

Like any other type of fraud, there are countless ways con artists can steal a mortgage or use a property that doesn't belong to them to make money. But there's one thing you can count on— mortgage fraud involves some form of impersonation. Whether that impersonation consists of all-out identity theft or a limited usurping of a person's identity to sign a paper or forge a document, some form of identity theft has occurred that appropriates the individual's name and robs a sense of security from that person.

MORTGAGE FRAUD SAFETY CHECKLIST

- Although there are exceptions, it should go without saying that you should actually view the home or property you are interested in before purchasing it.

- Ensure that no handwritten amendments are on your home's purchasing agreement.

- Be wary of a buyer who is willing to pay cash for the home and then attempts to place a large mortgage on the property.

- Be careful when buying a property from someone anxious to make a quick transaction; don't let anyone push you into making your decision before you are ready. Take your time and always move at your own speed.

- When purchasing a home, check out the sales history of that property. Have your lawyer conduct a title search, paying special attention to recent transfers, any unexplained increase in the property price and the names of lawyers on each transfer— the Law Society of Upper Canada notes that if the same lawyer is acting on behalf of each party in the transfer, it can be a red flag.

- Check out the credentials of the financial institution, mortgage broker, real estate agent and lawyer you are dealing with when purchasing or selling a home.

- Read all the documents before you sign anything.

- CMHC advises buyers to make sure they investigate if "anyone other than the seller has a financial interest in the home" they are thinking of purchasing.

- Never hand over the required deposit to the seller. This money should be held "In Trust" by "the Vendor's realty company or lawyer/notary."

- Never agree to be used as a straw buyer in a housing purchase— that means don't add your name to a mortgage unless you plan to buy that property.

- Always purchase title insurance on your home. In most cases it involves paying a one-time fee, and it stays in effect until you sell the property.

- If you inherit a home from a relative, make sure you have your own lawyer involved in every step of the process, and that any arrangements made between relatives in co-ownership of such a property are clearly spelled out.

Chapter Nine

Investment and Financial Fraud

~

WHEN IT SOUNDS TOO GOOD—IT USUALLY IS

I woke up one morning during the course of writing this book to discover that I had received yet another once-in-a-lifetime offer in my email inbox. This time it was the "Global WAZZUB Family" presenting me with a chance to get in on the "World's FIRST Profit Sharing Phenomenon."

According to the email, I didn't have to provide any money or personal information or perform any action other than register with the program. All I had to do was invite my lucky friends and acquaintances, whom I'm sure would thank me profusely for the consideration, to join the movement. The amount of money I would make in a given month would depend on the number of people I forwarded the email to—five friends who would return the favour by inviting five of their own friends, and that continues for five generations, and I would earn a monthly paycheque of $4000. If I was bold enough to send the email to 10 contacts and the same pyramid-pattern continued, my monthly income could "EXPLODE to $111,110 every month." And the good news just kept rolling in.

There was no limit to the number of people I could target while I sat back and watched my bank account grow.

Considering you're responsible for creating a "downline" of friends—individuals who you recruit and who in turn also register with this organization—suggests WAZZUB is a type of multi-level marketing (MLM) "opportunity." The increasing number of people who join these kinds of "opportunities" create, by default, a pyramid where the first individuals jumping on board potentially acquire the largest amount of money in the deal. This is also why some definitions of MLM marketing suggest it is akin to a pyramid scheme trying to look legitimate—a pyramid scheme is a "non-sustainable business model" that makes money off of individuals buying in to an idea, rather than by selling an actual product. Individuals at the top of the pyramid—those who originated or bought in early—see a return on their money but eventually no more people buy in and no money is left to pay those at the bottom of the pyramid. That said, the Competition Bureau of Canada does caution the public that some MLM opportunities are indeed legitimate business ventures—Amway is one example of a legitimate MLM business.

Because there are no clear directives disputing the legality of WAZZUB's intentions and the email recipient is not asked to share any personal information in order to register on the website, some folks might be enticed to try it out. After all, how was the request to forward the email any different from other email chain messages? How could you possibly lose?

There was one niggling factor. Some authorities suggest that a sense of urgency attached to an offer is a red flag when it comes to evaluating if an opportunity is valid or a scam. The offer I received gave me a deadline of April 9, 2012 to make a decision—10 days from the receipt of the email. Snooze and I would lose. That said, the company did demonstrate an effort at transparency by providing readers with one link to their company website and another to a You-Tube advertisement.

If you've read the previous pages in this book, by now you should be duly leery of clicking on any link in an unsolicited email. With that in mind, I took a few moments to Google WAZZUB on my web browser instead of clicking on the links within the email. I was surprised to discover dozens of chat sites and blogs discussing the WAZZUB phenomenon, and some of the writers suggested it might prove to be the next Google or Facebook in terms of international success and opportunities for financial reward.

Of course, other writers discounted those claims. One such dissident suggested WAZZUB was some mastermind's efforts at harvesting email addresses. Yet another implied the phenomenon could be a mass attempt at identity theft. And without a track record to review, both suggestions weren't out of the realm of possibility.

Based on the information I could gather, WAZZUB was in the "pre-launch" phase. After its official launch date of April 9, the people who've registered with the company are asked to set their default web homepage to WAZZUB. At that point, it's believed advertising will appear on the homepage, which will inevitably pay for the thousands of dollars being promised to registrants. Of course, it's impossible to predict if payments will indeed be made or whether the trusting souls who jumped on board in good faith will have been scammed.

Although a considerable amount of public commentary about this new "profit-sharing" scheme is available on the Internet, there is a stark absence of information from official channels. At the writing of this book, both the RCMP and the Canadian Anti-Fraud Centre had no information about WAZZUB on their websites. Further telephone calls to these organizations also came up empty.

So where does one go from here?

While some people may argue they have made large profits after getting on board early in a legitimate mass multi-level marketing scheme, others have not fared as well and some have lost large amounts of money. Still, the offer made by WAZZUB is free; you don't have to buy or sell anything, even after you register. And if you take precautions, as one writer suggested, by setting up an email address specifically for this purpose if you do decide to register, the result might be positive.

Questions surrounding the legitimacy of this "opportunity" most likely won't be answered until after the official launch, and perhaps not for many months beyond that date. In the end, each person has to decide for him or herself whether it is safe to take a chance on email offers like this one. For my money, or more importantly for my peace of mind, I'd stay away from these "opportunities." It may turn out that WAZZUB is legit, in which case I'll have missed my chance to make a bundle on the next big Internet craze. But if it is another scam, I'll know I didn't help to perpetrate it, nor will I have opened myself or any of my friends up to potential identity theft.

In 2011, various forms of financial fraud cost Canadians $650 million. Mortgage fraud is responsible for roughly $400 million of that total. Debit and credit card fraud, which makes up a smaller dollar amount in comparison to other frauds, affects more people.

In 2010, the Canadian Anti-Fraud Centre logged close to 50,000 complaints from various forms of investment-type fraud schemes that together cost Canadians a collective $50 million. The following sections focus on some of the more popular investment-type schemes, such as variations on the multi-level marketing promotion described above that con artists use to rid you of your hard-earned cash.

INSTANT CASH

The Better Business Bureau of Canada named advance fee loans as number two on its top 10 scams list for 2012. A variation of sorts on the Nigerian 419 email scam, where an individual is offered a "fee" to transfer large sums of money, advance fee loans scams promise guaranteed loans to needy recipients. However, these individuals are charged a processing fee for the service.

The advance fee loan scam isn't a new one, but it continues to draw unsuspecting victims. Perhaps one of the reasons for its success is how the loans are offered. In May 2001, a 31-year-old Toronto-area man was charged with fraud after he used this scam to allegedly collect an estimated $20,000 from his victims. The man attracted his victims, who were all Americans, through newspaper ads offering loans "to people with poor or no credit." These individuals were assured they had been approved for their loan, but in order to collect that money, they had to send an "insurance fee."

Of course, once that fee was submitted, these desperate individuals never saw a dime of the money they were promised. And now that they had sent the required insurance money, they were even more financially destitute than before.

There is never a time when an offer like this is legitimate. As the BBB explains, "it is illegal for a company to charge a fee in advance to obtain a loan, even if that fee is disguised as the first or last month's payment."

WHO CAN YOU TRUST?

To say it's a sad state of affairs is an understatement, but we've all heard stories about scams perpetrated in religious organizations by people who posed as leaders or who simply shared time in worship together. Perhaps more devastating are stories of friends and family members who've taken advantage of relational ties to turn a fast buck.

A fraud that targets members of a particular group is known as affinity fraud. Con artists bargain on the connection they share with the group, and they have a solid understanding of how to exploit that connection. They are able to successfully acquire investors because the offer has come from someone they know and trust or from someone from their social circle who they are comfortable with.

One of Canada's biggest affinity fraud cases involved Toronto's Ismaili community—and it all started with an infomercial in 2000.

Salim Mohammed Damji was a bit of a gambler. The 30-year-old had big dreams, and he was willing to jump through whatever hoops he had to in order to arrive at his desired destination in record time. Damji had dabbled in a few less-profitable schemes before stumbling upon an infomercial for a new tooth-whitening product called Instant White. The commercial resonated with him—Damji believed presenting oneself in a positive light was central to personal success— and he saw the white teeth and broad smiles flashing at him from his television screen as an opportunity to make some serious cash.

It would take an entire book to examine all the details involved in the affinity scam that resulted from Damji's chance viewing of that commercial. Suffice it to say that Damji claimed to own Strategic Trading Systems (the company name that sold Instant White) and began selling shares in the company to friends and family as well as the many acquaintances and businessmen who shared his Ismaili faith and worshipped with him. Damji offered investors a 20-to-one payoff on their investment. By the time the scam was exposed and Damji was in custody, the authorities estimated he had conned about 6000 people out of more than $75 million. And while that is a large number of victims and a lot of money, many of those victims were nickel and dimed to death, so to speak. According to a 2007 investor study commissioned by the Canadian Securities Administrators, fraud victims are not necessarily wealthy individuals. In fact, "one-third of fraud victims are scammed for less than $1000. Another 27 percent are taken for between $1000 and $5000." So the many people who lost small amounts of money to Damji were no less affected than those who, from their bigger resource pool, lost larger sums of money.

In the fall of 2011, affinity fraud was named one of the top five investment scams in Canada. A CBC report in November of that year cited the following statistics collected by the BC Securities Commission: an estimated one-half of all British Columbians had been approached to invest in a potentially fraudulent scam; only a quarter of those approached ever reported the incident; and "half of all fraud victims were preyed on by family or friend."

So the lesson here is that when it comes to parting with your money, don't blindly trust anyone—not even your own family or close friends.

FOREX Scams

The online investment dictionary InvestorWords.com defines FOREX (short for "foreign exchange market") as an "over-the-counter market where buyers and sellers conduct foreign exchange transactions." FOREX investments simplify transactions between countries, making them an attractive trading option. They also allow "an investment opportunity for risk-seeking investors who don't mind engaging in speculation."

It's precisely because of the risks involved in this kind of investment that specially trained professionals are required to competently execute the tasks involved in the financial venture. These professionals are usually employed by large international banks and make use of the best technology available in order to make money in this highly unpredictable market.

Advertisements placed in various media outlets make the opportunity sound exotic and exciting, with promises of huge payouts for a seemingly simple transaction. The Canadian Securities Administrators (CSA) warn that the ads look professional, and usually come in the guise of providing a service, such as offering readers a chance to directly invest "on the foreign exchange…market," or to assist them in their decision-making by selling them software or providing courses on the topic. The problem is that once a potential investor sends money, it is quite often the end of the transaction. Many of these would-be investors never receive the software or the promised schooling they paid for, and any money they sent for investment purposes all too frequently ends up in the pockets of a scam artist. And while software programs and trading courses might help to educate potential shareholders on trading trends, they can't help to accurately predict how the value of any particular currency might change and as such shouldn't be relied upon for guidance in such risky investments. The CSA states that at best, "more than 70 per cent of the FOREX market is speculative."

On March 29, 2012, the CSA issued an investor watch, warning Canadians of "an increase in foreign exchange…trading services being offered to investors in Canada, by both Canadian as well as foreign firms." If you are determined to take a chance on the FOREX market, the CSA advises that the best way to safeguard your money is to get the advice of a registered financial professional. They also warn investors to make sure that the dealer you are thinking of investing with is not the counterparty to your trade; since only one of you will benefit from the transaction, your potential loss will be the dealer's gain, creating a conflict of interest.

Steer clear of anyone offering a low-risk, high-return guarantee on a FOREX market—this is without a doubt a scam. Transparency in all your investment interactions is a financial best practice and FOREX trading is no different. Be wary of dealers or brokers who don't want to share their past track record with you or who aren't registered with their regional securities commission.

PENNY AUCTIONS

Imagine landing a brand-new GPS for $5, a Starbucks $50 gift card for 80 cents or a KitchenAid mixer for $7. These items represent what one online penny auction participant claims were his most successful experiences in the bidding circle. But as I've mentioned many times in this book, when something looks too good to be true, it usually is. When it comes to penny auctions, for every good-news story there are a lot of people with lighter wallets. In fact, unless you only bid on a single auction and win that auction at a low price, you will always lose some money on the gamble.

Penny auctions, also known as bidding fee auctions, are often disguised as a news report or legitimate-looking advertisement telling readers of amazing deals on retail gift cards or larger items such as iPads or laptop computers. For only pennies on the dollar, a winner could walk away with an awesome deal.

Penny auctions take place on websites where a select number of items are displayed at any given time, complete with their value, their current bid and a running time clock letting bidders know how long they have to place their bids. While rules differ from one site to another, bidders usually purchase their bids in bundles of 100 or more, and requests for minimum bids aren't unusual, as well as non-refundable subscription fees. But unlike other auctions, you don't merely lose your item if you don't have the winning bid—you lose all the money you've bid. For example, if you bid $1999 on a car that sold for $2000, you'd be on the hook for the $1999. You're basically being charged for the chance of buying something!

Smaller items can be won for as little as five dollars or less, which you might argue is affordable if you lose the bid. However, participation in these auctions can be addicting; penny auctions have been criticized for being nothing more than another online gambling option. Participants can bid on a number of items at one time, and an intensity naturally builds as the clock counts down its last few seconds, only to have more seconds added with every additional bid. It's important to recognize that there are always more losers than winners. Over time, the losses add up and sometimes surpass the value of the item that was on the bidding block in the first place.

That said, penny auctions are a great deal for the auctioneer. Even when a valuable item is auctioned off for a fraction of its worth, the auctioneer can pull in many times more than its true value because every bid from every client, win or lose, is money in the auctioneer's pocket. That new car might have sold for $2000, but the potentially thousands of bidders who lost still have to pay for the bids they made.

In addition to the dangers of getting carried away by the penny auction experience, there are many scam sites out there. While some victims might end up swallowing a loss because they may not have been aware they were scammed, others can spot a scam and aren't so willing to say "uncle."

That's exactly what happened to a 24-year-old Alberta resident named Jesse Willms. The Sherwood Park "entrepreneur" outraged enough customers who recognized they were scammed that he found himself in a battle with the U.S. Federal Trade Commission (FTC) on charges of online fraud. According to a Sun Media report dated February 24, 2012, penny auctions were just one of the ways Willms enticed his alleged victims. The FTC charged that the 11 companies Willms operated "lured consumers in the U.S. and other countries with 'free' trial offers for weight-loss pills, teeth whiteners, health supplements, and work-at-home scheme, access to government grants, free credit reports and penny auctions." Willms allegedly made his many millions by using a practice called "negative-option marketing." For example, Willms offered customers a "free trial," but unless they formally requested to discontinue their association, the free offer ended up costing them $79.98 every month, or more if additional fees for "bonus offers" were added on.

While Willms did not admit to violating any laws in his case, he did agree to a $359-million settlement. He is also no longer allowed to use negative-option marketing in any of his business dealings.

~

INVESTMENT FRAUD CHECKLIST

- First, ask yourself if the proposed investment makes sense and whether the promised return is too good to be true. If your gut tells you it's a ridiculous windfall, back away immediately.

- Check, check and recheck investment options before jumping on board with what looks like a great opportunity a friend or acquaintance has shared with you. Your mother told you to do your homework for a reason—it will save your personal and financial health.

- Contact the Securities Commission office in your area to ensure the individual trying to sell you an investment is actually licensed to do so.

News Alert:
Investor Beware

Gilles Dube, an 81-year-old Catholic priest posing as a psychiatrist, was one of three individuals charged with defrauding an Alberta doctor out of $500,000 between April 1 and July 31, 2006. Dube, Jean Pierre Belleuille and Jamie Jie Tong Yu, the men allegedly involved in the scheme, posed as doctors looking for investors to assist them in opening medical clinics in Calgary and British Columbia. In 2011, con artist and co-conspirator Belleuille received a six-year prison sentence for his part in the investment scam.

- Read through Investor Warning Lists on Securities Commission websites to make sure the company you're considering doing business with isn't flagged on that site.

- Make sure there is no conflict of interest with the party offering you the investment. For example, the person connecting you with a potential investment must not have any personal connection to that investment.

- The Ontario Securities Commission warns investors to also "check for both concluded and ongoing disciplinary proceedings against individuals and firms." You can do this through the Canadian

Securities Administrators (CSA), the Mutual Fund Dealers Association of Canada (MFDA), the Investment Industry Regulatory Organization of Canada (IIROC) and the Ontario Securities Commission (OSC) or your provincial counterpart; all maintain separate databases.

- Ask to see the prospectus—the document outlining the details of the investment opportunity, including stocks, bonds and mutual funds, as well as information on the business you are thinking of dealing with, such as their financial statements, the list and biographies of officers serving on the board of directors, and so on. And once you get this prospectus in your hands, read it thoroughly.

- Contact the other financial institutions and companies that are involved in the same investment to double-check the information you find in the prospectus.

- Spend the necessary money to get second and third opinions from financial advisors and have your lawyer and accountant review the information.

- Get any guarantee in writing but, as the Ontario Securities Commission states, "a guarantee is only as good as the person or company offering it."

- Always make sure whomever you are dealing with does not employ negative-option marketing techniques.

- Read the fine print in any financial document that you are asked to sign.

~

Chapter Ten

Identity Theft: More to the Story

~

There is nothing straightforward about how identity theft and fraud work. The steps involved aren't necessarily sequential at all times. For example, the criminal who is plotting ways to steal your mail isn't necessarily the same person who potentially wants to assume your good name and credit history. As with any aspect of law, there are degrees of collusion and manipulation, and the slippery slope that lands someone in jail on charges of identity theft isn't always what one might expect.

To this point in this book, I've examined how, for the most part, identities are stolen to procure some kind of financial reward—someone pretends to be you to access your money and gain the power and prestige they believe money can buy. But the criminal who initially accesses the personal information necessary to steal an identity isn't always the same person responsible for raiding a victim's accounts or initiating the sequence of events that leads to full-scale identity theft. Sometimes the person responsible for stealing mail from your mailbox, for example, is merely a bottom feeder in the criminal world. Their job is to provide information in exchange for fast cash—money that, in many cases, is used to support a drug habit. The following stories examine how drug addiction is often one motivating force behind identity theft.

THE DRUG CONNECTION: IDENTITY THEFT ADDS TO COST OF ADDICTION

A story coming out of Port Orchard, Washington, in March 2004 has the makings of a good police TV drama: sex, drugs, money and multiple criminal infractions. But police weren't looking for that when they knocked on a truck window to speak to the driver.

The long and intricate investigation started when police pulled up alongside a parked truck at a mobile home park just outside of the town. People in parked vehicles always raise a few eyebrows for the authorities—you never know what mischief might be going on. Most often that "mischief" is fairly minor when compared with some of the more serious situations law enforcement officials find themselves up against on any given shift. Still, the officers on duty that night had to check it out. They needed to make sure everything was okay—when it comes to police work, you never know what you might discover.

As it turned out, the events of that night kept officers at the precinct talking for a very long time.

When they approached the parked truck, police found two stark-naked individuals surrounded by piles of mail. None of the correspondence littering the truck cab was addressed to either of its occupants. The mail, the two startled and embarrassed culprits were quick to admit, was stolen—but they had no intention of keeping it. Instead, they planned to trade the mail for drugs—methamphetamine in particular—from a dealer at a nearby mobile home.

Using the directions provided by the two panicked characters in the truck, police arrived at the trailer to find more than someone selling drugs. They discovered a small methamphetamine lab, along with an assortment of stolen goods, including more mail and "notebooks with handwritten notations about fraudulent transactions and printouts of stolen identity data." Detective Jerry Jensen told msnbc.com correspondent Bob Sullivan that the individuals in the home were "drugged out of their minds."

"They lived like pigs," Jensen said. "It was a house full of stolen stuff and it's all about meth."

The connection between methamphetamine addiction and identity theft was already being tracked and documented by the time this story hit the news, and the trend hasn't let up over the intervening years.

A *USA Today* article highlighting an Edmonton story penned by Byron Acohido and Jon Swartz explained that, "Identity theft has fast become the crime of preference among meth users for three reasons: it is non-violent, criminal penalties for first-time offenders are light—usually a few days or weeks in jail—and the use of computers and the Internet offers crooks anonymity and speed with which to work."

They go on to explain that meth addicts are the perfect guinea pigs to use in this kind of criminal enterprise. Their drug of choice is highly addictive and "turns users into automatons willing to take on risky, street-level crime." Meth also gives these "human robots" endless amounts of energy—energy they can then invest into hacking into computer databases full of personal information.

In 2005, the city of Edmonton was home base to an international identity theft and methamphetamine ring that no longer "relied solely on dumpster-diving, mailbox-pilfering street addicts to supply stolen credit cards, checks and account statements...it had advanced to complex joint ventures, conducted over the Internet, in partnership with organized cybercrime rings outside the country."

The *USA Today* report outlined how Edmonton Police Service detectives Bob Gauthier and Al Vonkeman discovered the network's shabby headquarters in a rent-by-the-hour motel in the city's downtown core in the winter of 2005. The officers had been hot on the heels of several suspects involved in the case for more than two years. Each time police thought they'd pinpointed the place these individuals operated from, the suspects moved elsewhere. An RCMP press release on the incident explained that the culprits were difficult to locate because of their vast computer knowledge. In particular, they "made use of Voice Over Internet Protocol (VOIP) Internet phone services that permit the user to choose any area code, thereby, masking their location."

This time, in 2005, the officers were lucky: they managed to snag the two men they believed were responsible for linking "outside crime groups" to stolen account information the pair had managed to collect and store. The officers also had enough information to wend their way through a spiderweb of global connections—and effectively take a bite out of identity theft crime.

The efforts of these officers, though remarkably successful, only represent the mere tip of the iceberg when it comes to the connection between identity theft and drugs. And instead of success stories like these discouraging other thieves from procuring stolen documents for the purposes of identity theft, the problem continues to grow.

In 2009, a police investigation into what *Edmonton Sun* reporter Richard Liebrecht called "a sophisticated identity theft ring benefiting methamphetamine users" discovered more than 120 victims who'd had their accounts drained, unauthorized charges placed on their credit cards and unsanctioned accounts opened in their names.

According to Edmonton City Police Acting Detective David Butt, personal information from these victims, which was often stolen from gym lockers and vehicles, was used as a "form of currency among the ID theft ring partners and meth users." After police connected their suspect to a storage locker "that contained boxes filled with hundreds of stolen documents, including health care cards, passports and credit cards," police felt they had enough evidence to issue an arrest warrant in March 2010.

Six months after their warrant was made public, police finally arrested a 25-year-old Edmonton man and meth user, David Shawn Tidman. By the time Tidman was captured, he faced almost 150 charges but pleaded guilty to only 17 of those charges for "fraud-related crimes committed between 2008 and 2010." He was sentenced to a 20-month jail term for his offences.

Another more recent investigation involving a combination of identity theft and drug trafficking resulted in the February 2012 arrest of a 29-year-old Winnipeg man who was facing almost 200 related charges. At this writing, the Winnipeg case remains before the courts.

Stories like the ones described above are all too common. However, officials now have a deeper awareness of what motivates some criminals to commit identity theft. And the public has an understanding of the desperation propelling some ID thieves to risk everything to steal their mail.

Identity theft is a trend that the RCMP suggests will continue, for several reasons. They explain that crimes like mail theft are a "low-tech and highly effective crime used to acquire personal information to commit identity fraud." Simply put, it doesn't take much cunning or ability to lift someone's mail, even from a locked box.

In addition, criminals with Internet and computer skills have the ability to access personal information while tucked away in an unknown location, making it even more difficult for the authorities to identify and arrest the culprits involved. As always, the best ammunition against identity theft is to educate yourself on the safety measures to take in order to protect your personal information.

PROTECT YOUR ID WHILE TRAVELLING

It's easy to get so caught up in the excitement of a long-awaited trip that we let our guard down. Identity thieves watch for travellers laughing with friends and family over dinner, or lolling on the beach, soaking up the sun's warmth. Attentive to your every move, these thieves know just when to pounce on personal items left out in plain sight and score your credit card or other documents.

In fact, perpetrators of this kind of crime are so skilled in their field that they can even manage to victimize the authorities. The next recent story is a highly publicized American example, but it is so shockingly textbook that I had to include it in this collection.

John Sileo of Denver, Colorado, took his daughter on a business trip to Orlando, Florida. Since his work responsibilities took him to the home of Disney World, Sileo capitalized on the opportunity to take his daughter for a visit to the theme park. But Sileo's day of fun and adventure ended on a sour note when he received an unexpected telephone call from his bank, notifying him that his credit card had been shut down.

Thankfully, Sileo had all the right security measures in place should he ever fall victim to possible identity theft. And the security measures alerted his credit card company of the sudden strange online shopping charges—$3000 worth.

Sileo had all the tools to protect himself from being victimized. As an identity theft and fraud expert with CSID, a company specializing in identity protection innovation, Sileo was careful, especially when he travelled. Sileo estimated that he spends as many as 50 days every year on business trips—ironically, during his Orlando trip, he was giving a speech to the Treasury Department on ways to avoid identity theft.

Despite Sileo's expertise in the field, a sly thief managed to find a way to pilfer information to rack up Sileo's credit card with unauthorized purchases. Sileo told reporters that he believed the culprit responsible "used a smartphone to snap a picture of his card number at the theme park's electronic ticket booth." Still, it's precisely because of Sileo's expertise that the theft of his credit card number was recognized, his account shut down, and any further damage to his name and finances averted.

Attempts to steal your identity can also happen on the home front while you're enjoying a vacation. Unattended homes, with mail and flyers piling up in mailboxes, are sure signs that residents are away. So are social media status updates.

Vacationers have been targeted after updating their statuses in an effort to keep in contact with friends and family members back home. Your online presence is one more thing to consider when protecting yourself from identity theft.

TRAVEL SAFETY CHECKLIST

Here are other ideas to keep your identity safe while on holiday:

- Inform your credit card providers of your travel destination and the length of time you expect to be away.

- Always use your credit card instead of a debit card to book hotels, vehicle rentals and other travel arrangements—using a credit card decreases your liability should someone compromise your transaction.

- Have your mail and newspapers collected on a regular basis while you are away, or consider having the post office put a hold on your mail deliveries.

- Make sure you have someone mow your lawn, shovel your sidewalk or do any other necessary home maintenance while you are away. Another option is to hire a house-sitter during your absence.

- Do not share your vacation experiences on social media networks until after you return from vacation. Distant acquaintances or friends of friends might have access to that information and your home could be a target for thieves. Would-be identity thieves can scour your unattended home, looking for personal information such as bank statements, birth certificates, Social Insurance

Numbers and other important documents. Service Canada is doing their part to prevent loss or theft of SIN cards by phasing them out altogether, starting in 2014.

- Financial education specialists Investopedia suggest that if you do a lot of travelling, you should consider purchasing a laptop to use exclusively while you are on the road if you can afford it. But refrain from using this laptop to do any banking or other personal business. That way, should you lose your computer or it is stolen, the amount of information the thief can access is limited.

- Always be aware of your surroundings when you travel, which includes watching people who might be hovering too close while you are making any financial transaction. As evidenced in the above story, cellphone cameras can be used to snap pictures of your credit cards during transactions.

- Shield your card and your personal identification number when making a transaction.

- Don't leave your restaurant receipt on an unattended table, especially if it contains your signature. As one expert pointed out in a WAFF 48 television news broadcast, your signature is one more piece in "the puzzle they [identity thieves] might need to steal your identity."

- Some experts suggest you use a money belt instead of a wallet or purse to carry your important documents. Or better still, secure your private documents, such as your passport, in a hotel security deposit box until you require them again—large chain hotels often offer this security to their customers.

- Don't travel with more than two credit cards—lock one in the hotel safe as a backup card and carry one with you. That limits the amount of damage a potential thief can do if your wallet or purse is stolen, and at the same time you aren't left without any resources for yourself.

- Some business travellers have invested in smartphones that can have their contents erased remotely should the traveller ever lose the phone. There is an added cost for this option, but one you might want to consider if you do a lot of travelling.

- Be wary of anyone requesting information by telephone. Some travellers have fallen victim to criminals who've called their hotel room with an alleged emergency query about a problem processing your credit card number. Some travellers didn't give the request a second thought and gave the number, only to find they'd given their information to a thief. Instead, hang up the phone and go to the hotel's front desk and speak directly to a customer service employee.

One final suggestion you may want to consider when planning a vacation is to buy travel insurance that includes protection against identity theft. In fact, many specialists suggest that identity-theft insurance is as important as any other insurance you purchase.

The next section reviews some of your insurance options, the names of Canadian companies that provide identity-theft coverage and what you should look for in a policy.

55

BUYING PEACE OF MIND

So, what if you know the risks out there and do everything you can to protect yourself, and you still fall victim to identity theft, just as John Sileo did in the above story? Aside from educating yourself and taking preventative measures, what more can you do?

The question of purchasing identity-theft insurance to cover you should you experience a devastating situation stirs up considerable debate. When it comes to weighing the pros and cons, it's not always clear if the insurance is worth the money spent on it. And are there so many exceptions and loopholes to the insurance coverage that should you need to use it you'll find you get very little out of it?

It's an argument many wage over all kinds of insurance coverage. And it's a good idea to get objective advice on the type of home, vehicle and life insurance one should purchase at any given moment in your life so that you can purchase the best policy for you and your family—one that will provide you with the coverage and peace of mind you deserve.

When it comes to protecting yourself against a crime that, although fairly new, is one of the "fastest growing crimes in Canada," doing your homework is especially important. What does each insurance carrier promise with his or her particular plan? Will they restore your ruined credit rating if it's been abused? What happens to the money you would lose taking time off work to get the help you need, or to potentially appear in court? Does your policy pay for some of that lost time? Or does your insurance company provide an employee to make the contacts necessary to do that for you?

Toronto Dominion Bank's identity theft coverage, the Identity Plus Advantage, is one example of what an insurance provider offers. It boasts a no-deductible product that provides victims of identity theft with a "case manager" who works to "restore your credit and your reputation." However, there are limits—as with any kind of coverage. The company's website promises the case manager will deal with "most of the relevant authorities on your behalf." What isn't clear through the website is exactly what this means. Who will they contact, and what organizations are beyond their purview? Most insurance providers will include statements like this in their coverage documents, but it's important you have a representative spell out what exactly they mean—what is and is not being covered? How much in lost wages can you expect to be compensated for? Ask every question that comes to mind before following through with the purchase.

In most cases, insurance providers do not reimburse bank accounts and credit cards compromised as a result of identity theft. That is typically the responsibility of the financial institution and credit card providers. But to make sure you are covered, contact the companies you deal with to find out their policies. Most financial institutions cover losses that are the result of identity theft and identity fraud, provided the incident is reported in a timely fashion.

Another way of protecting yourself against the damage an identity thief can potentially cause is to sign up for monthly credit reports from Equifax or TransUnion. You will be charged a nominal fee for the coverage, but it provides you with a peace of mind. The monitoring service allows you to protect yourself and recover from the monetary losses that are all too common should someone use your name and personal information to access money, or open and maximize accounts you haven't authorized.

Final Words

The research and writing of this book spawned many discussions on the subject of identity theft and its resulting fraud. Some tidbits of information proved to be eye opening to certain individuals while others I spoke with provided new angles for me to pursue.

At one point in the penning of this book I found myself rambling on with a colleague about all the dangers surrounding email correspondence. "Snail mail isn't much better," I said, explaining how easy it is for a criminal to lift mail from unlocked mailboxes and uncover key information that can open the doors to stealing a person's identity.

"Yes, well, one can get carried away with the paranoia," she said. I was a tad put out initially, especially considering this individual was involved in this project, if only on the periphery. Why was I working on this project if my enthusiasm was verging on paranoia?

But she had a point. Examine any topic where self-improvement or self-awareness is involved and there is a fine line between a healthy examination and dysfunctional neurosis. This book is not intended to paralyze you with an unhealthy fear, or have you looking over your shoulder at every turn. It is meant to provide you, the reader, with information that is crucial for your personal safety and well-being. As Stephen Covey so eloquently once said, "Every human has four endowments—self-awareness, conscience, independent will and creative imagination. These give us the ultimate human freedom…. The power to choose, to respond, to change."

Glossary

Affinity fraud: Fraud schemes that attack a particular social group, such as seniors, the disabled or members of a particular church or organization.

Brand spoofing: Email correspondence that looks official, complete with company names, logos and letterheads. Banking institutions and PayPal are frequently spoofed this way, but similar techniques could also be used to mirror retail outlets using email correspondence to inform customers of upcoming sales. The goal is to have recipients open the email and click on the link provided.

Confidence trick: A fraud committed once the con artist gains a victim's trust and confidence.

Financial fraud: The Winnipeg Police Service names financial fraud as the "most common form of identity theft." A criminal steals your identity, if only for brief periods of time, in order to easily steal your money.

FOREX: An "over-the-counter market where buyers and sellers conduct foreign exchange transactions" (from InvestorWords.com).

Ghosting: Commonly defined as "a form of identity theft whereby an individual assumes the identity of a deceased individual." (*See* Tombstoning)

Hacker: A cyber thief who gains unauthorized access to a computer.

Identity fraud: The RCMP Commercial Crime Branch (CCB) defines identity fraud as "the actual deceptive use of the identity information of another person (living or dead) in connection with various frauds (including for example personating another person and the misuse of debit card or credit card data)."

Identity theft: The RCMP CCB defines identity theft as "the preparatory stage of acquiring and collecting someone else's personal information for criminal purposes."

Keystroke logging: Occurs when a program or individual is able to connect through your computer's back door and, unbeknownst to the owner, monitor each keystroke as it's being typed.

Lebanese loop: A strip of metal or plastic attached inside an ATM card slot and capable of reading the card. Once the owner finishes inputting their PIN and receiving their cash, this gadget prevents the card from being ejected.

Malware: A shorthand name for malicious software that can include viruses, worms and many other methods of attacking computer systems. A virus is a computer program that, once installed, can do varying degrees of damage to your system. This malicious program can replicate itself and attach itself to "other storage media such as USB keys or external hard drives." The RCMP defines a worm as a "self-replicating program that resides in memory (RAM) and in most cases does not alter files on the hard drive. It propagates by sending itself to other computers in a network." Worms, such as Code Red, released onto the Internet on July 13, 2001, can crash entire networks and cause millions of dollars in damage.

Payment card fraud: Using another person's identity in order to gain access to that individual's credit card or bank account information and make unauthorized transactions.

Penny auctions: Also known as bidding fee auctions, penny auctions are online auctions where bidders bid up by the penny. While it seems like a small fee, those bids add up, and unlike live auctions, where only the winning bid pays, everyone who takes part in a penny auction has to pay out their bid. Players are basically being charged for the chance of buying something.

Pharming: Pharming occurs when a hacker taps into a Domain Name System's server in order to redirect traffic from a legitimate website to a bogus website. By pharming, or DNS poisoning, a hacker can collect personal information without raising any suspicion and empty victims' bank accounts before they ever realize their personal information was compromised.

Phishing: Phishing attempts come in the form of spam email messages that look official and contain letterhead and contact information that appear to come from a bank or accounts-based business, such as PayPal. The goal of this form of spam is to collect personal information. Once collected, this information can be used to empty victims' bank accounts, or steal their identity.

Pop-up ads: Annoying ads that pop up on the Internet out of nowhere. They are more irritating than dangerous. Some of them, however, can launch spyware on your computer and disrupt your online interactions.

Pyramid scheme: a "non-sustainable business model" that makes money off of individuals buying in to an idea, rather than by selling an actual product.

Radio Frequency Identification (RFID): *PC Magazine* defines RFID as "a data collection technology that uses electronic tags for storing data. The tag...is made up of an RFID chip attached to an antenna. Transmitting in the kilohertz, megahertz and gigahertz ranges, tags may be battery-powered or derive their power from the RF waves coming from the reader."

Service scam: A scam that usually involves a telephone call where "any false, deceptive or misleading promotion of services or solicitation for services" is promoted and often includes "offers for telecommunications, internet, finance, medical and energy services" as well as "extended warranties, insurance and sales service." Notice that the "services" being offered are what most of us would consider among life's necessities, such as medical care, electricity, insurance and so on.

Spam: Unwanted email arriving in your inbox. Typically, these messages are distributed to huge numbers of recipients, and many of these addresses have been purchased. Most of these messages, or "spam," contain some kind of advertisement or pornographic material.

Spyware: Software that "spies" on an individual with the purpose of collecting personal information without someone's knowledge. Sometimes spyware is included in free shareware products downloaded from the Internet, and the information collected creates "marketing profiles" that help advertising companies improve their marketing campaigns. Spyware is not illegal, and quite often Internet users agree to having their habits monitored without realizing it because they haven't fully read the licence agreement they have downloaded.

Tombstoning: The collecting of names and histories of recently deceased individuals from obituaries and graveyards, for example, in order to create new identities.

Trojan Horse: If a computer virus spreads with the voracity of a bacterial virus, a Trojan Horse is as deceptive and imposing as its name suggests. Typically, a Trojan Horse disguises itself as what looks like a harmless attachment with extensions such as .exe, .bat, .pif, .com and .vbs. But if you double-click on that attachment it will run a program on your computer that can destroy files or allow a hacker complete access to your computer. The RCMP warns that once a Trojan Horse is executed, it can "copy and delete files or use your computer as a stepping stone to hack other computers. They can even watch you via your Web cam!"

Appendix

Resources

The focus of this book is to provide you with as much information as possible to arm you against falling victim to identity theft and fraud. To that end, make it a personal policy to check out any businesses or charities you want to do business with before making a purchase or donating money. One of the best ways of checking out the legitimacy of businesses or charities is by logging on to the Canadian Council of Better Business Bureaus' national site or the regional site in your province. The BBB evaluates the performance and integrity of businesses and charities registered with the organization and provides that information to consumers so they can make educated decisions about becoming involved with any of these companies. As well, BBB receives and investigates consumer complaints. The national and provincial offices are listed below.

Should you find you have become a victim of identity theft or fraud, it is crucial that you connect with the appropriate authorities that can help you minimize the damage to your name, finances and credit, and monitor any ongoing unwanted activities. Those organizations and their contact numbers are also included below.

BETTER BUSINESS BUREAUS
Canadian Council of Better Business Bureaus
www.bbb.org/Canada/

Alberta Offices
BBB of Central and Northern Alberta
16102-100 Avenue NW
Edmonton, AB T5K 2L9
Phone: 780-488-6632
24-hour info line: 780-482-2341
Consumer Consultants (Complaints & Information)
Monday to Thursday, 8:30 AM to 4:00 PM (780-482-2341)
Toll-free Line: 1-800-232-7298 (nationwide, 24 hours/day)
Fax: 780-482-1150
Email: info@edmontonbbb.org

Calgary BBB (Southern Alberta and East Kootenays)
350 7330 Fisher Street SE
Calgary, AB T2H 2H8
General information: 403-531-8784, info@calgary.bbb.org
Inquiries/complaints: 403-517-4222, complaints@calgary.bbb.org
Fax: 403-640-2514

Lethbridge Office
416-10 Street North
Lethbridge, AB T1H 2C7
Email: info@lethbridge.bbb.org
Phone: 403-394-0660
Toll-free Phone: 1-855-394-0660
Fax: 403-394-0669

Medicine Hat Office (call for appointment)
PO Box 302, 97 Carry Drive
Medicine Hat, AB T1B 3M6
Email: info@medicinehat.bbb.org
Phone: 403-527-6484
Toll free: 1-855-394-0660

British Columbia
Better Business Bureau of Mainland BC
Suite 404, 788 Beatty Street
Vancouver, BC V6B 2M1
Office hours: 9:00 AM to 4:00 PM
Website: www.mbc.bbb.org

Better Business Bureau of Vancouver Island
#220-1175 Cook Street
Victoria, BC V8V 4A1
Phone: 250-386-6348
Toll free: 1-877-826-4222
Fax: 250-386-2367
Office hours: 9:00 AM to 4:00 PM, Monday to Friday
General inquiries: info@vi.bbb.org
Complaints: complaints@vi.bbb.org
Questions about BBB Accreditation: business@vi.bbb.org

Better Business Bureau of Saskatchewan Inc.

980 Albert Street

Regina, SK S4R 2P7

Phone: 306-352-7601

Toll free: 888-352-7601 (in Saskatchewan only)

Fax: 306-565-6236

Better Business Bureau of Manitoba and Northwest Ontario

B-1030 Empress Street

Winnipeg, MB R3G 3H4

Phone: 204-989-9010

Fax: 204-989-9016

Toll free: 1-800-385-3074

BBB Mid-Western and Central Ontario

Main Office:

354 Charles Street E

Kitchener, ON N2G 4L5

Phone: 519-579-3080

Toll Free: 1-800-459-8875

Fax: 519-570-0072

Business Office:

1 Eva Rd

Toronto, ON M9C 4Z5

Accreditation services: 416-621-09184

Inquiries: 416-323-9946

BBB Western Ontario

Mailing address:

PO Box 2153

London, ON N6A 4E3

Office:

308-200 Queens Avenue

London, ON N6A 1J3

Phone: 519-673-3222

Toll free: (519 area only): 1-877-283-9222

General information: info@westernontario.bbb.org

Complaints: complaints@westernontario.bbb.org

Member services: memberservices@westernontario.bbb.org

Hours of operation: Monday to Friday, 8:30 AM to 4:30 PM

General inquiries & Complaints: Monday to Friday, 9:00 AM to 4:00 PM

BBB Windsor and Southwestern Ontario

Canadian Consumer Information Gateway—Office of Consumer
Affairs Industry Canada

235 Queen Street, 6th Floor West

Ottawa, ON K1A 0H5

Phone: 613-946-2576

Email: consumer.information@ic.gc.ca

BBB Eastern and Northern Ontario and the Outaouais

700 Industrial Avenue, Unit 505

Ottawa, ON K1G 0Y9

Phone: 613-237-4856

Fax: 613-237-4878

General inquiries: info@ottawa.bbb.org

Québec Commercial Certification Office Inc.
Centre d'affaire de l'Avenir
1565, boul. de l'Avenir, bureau #206
Laval, PQ H7S 2N5
Phone: 514-905-3893
Fax: 450-663-6316
Email: info@occq-qcco.com

Better Business Bureau Serving the Atlantic Provinces
1888 Brunswick Street, Suite 805
Halifax, NS B3J 3J8
For HRM (a service for the hearing impaired): 422-6581
For the rest of the Atlantic provinces: 1-877-663-2363
Fax: 902-429-6457
Email: bbbmp@bbbmp.ca

ROYAL CANADIAN MOUNTED POLICE
Scam and Fraud Division
RCMP National Headquarters
Headquarters Building
73 Leikin Drive
Ottawa, ON K1A 0R2
General inquiries: 613-993-7267
TTY: 613-993-2232
Fax: 613-993-0260
Website: www.rcmp-grc.gc.ca

CANADIAN ANTI-FRAUD CENTRE
Box 686

North Bay, ON P1B 8J8

Hours of operation: Monday to Friday, 8:30 AM to 4:30 PM

Phone: 705-495-8501

Toll-free fax: 1-888-654-9426

Website: www.antifraudcentre.ca

Email: info@antifraudcentre.ca

OFFICE OF THE PRIVACY COMMISSIONER OF CANADA
112 Kent Street, Place de Ville

Tower B, 3rd Floor

Ottawa, ON K1A 1H3

Toll free: 1-800-282-1376

Phone: 613-947-1698

Fax: 613-947-6850

TTY: 613-992-9190

INDUSTRY CANADA, OFFICE OF CONSUMER AFFAIRS
Industry Canada Web Service Centre

C.D. Howe Building

235 Queen Street

Ottawa, ON K1A 0H5

Business hours: Monday to Friday, 8:30 AM to 5:00 PM

Phone: 613-954-5031

Toll free: 1-800-328-6189

Fax: 613-954-2340

TTY: 1-866-694-8389

Website: www.ic.gc.ca

EQUIFAX CANADA INC.

5650 Yonge Street
Toronto, ON M2M 4G3
Phone: 1-855-233-9226
Email: webleads@equifax.com
Business hours: Monday to Saturday, 9:00 AM to 5:00 PM
Website: www.consumer.equifax.ca/home/en_ca

TRANSUNION CANADA
All provinces except Québec

TransUnion Consumer Relations
PO Box 338, LCD1
Hamilton, ON L8L 7W2
Toll free: 1-800-663-9980
Website: www.transunion.ca

Québec residents

TransUnion Centre De Relations Aux Consommateurs
TransUnion 1 Place Laval
Ouest Suite 370
Laval, PQ H7N 1A1
Phone: 514-335-0374
Toll free: 1-877-713-3393

SECURITY COMMISSIONS
Alberta Securities Commission
Suite 600, 250-5th Street SW
Calgary, AB T2P 0R4
Business hours: Monday to Friday, 8:00 AM to 5:00 PM
Public inquiries: 403-355-4151
Complaints: 403-355-3888
Fax: 403-297-6156
Toll free: 1-877-355-0585

British Columbia Securities Commission
701 West Georgia Street
PO Box 10142, Pacific Centre
Vancouver, BC V7Y 1L2
Phone: 604-899-6854
Toll free: 1-800-373-6393
Fax: 604-899-6506

Manitoba Securities Commission
500-400 St. Mary Avenue
Winnipeg, MB R3C 4K5
Phone: 204-945-2548
Toll free: 1-800-655-5244 (Manitoba only)
Fax: 204-945-0330
Email: securities@gov.mb.ca

Manitoba Securities Commission Real Estate Division
500-400 St. Mary Avenue
Winnipeg, MB R3C 4K5
Phone: 204-945-2562
Fax: 204-948-4627
Email: realestate@gov.mb.ca

New Brunswick Securities Commission
Suite 300, 85 Charlotte Street
Saint John, NB E2L 2J2
Reception: 506-658-3060
Fax: 506-658-3059
Toll free: 1-866-933-2222 (within province)
Email: information@nbsc-cvmnb.ca

Nova Scotia Securities Commission
2nd Floor, Joseph Howe Building
1690 Hollis Street
Halifax, NS B3J 3J9
Phone: 902-424-7768
Toll free (within province): 1-855-424-2499
Fax: 902-424-4625
Website: www.gov.ns.ca/nssc/

Ontario Securities Commission
20 Queen Street West, Suite 1903
Toronto, ON M5H 3S8
Business hours: Monday to Friday, 8:30 AM to 5:00 PM
Phone: 416-593-8314
Toll free: 1-877-785-1555
TTY: 1-866-827-1295
Fax: 416-593-8122
Email: inquiries@osc.gov.on.ca

Prince Edward Island Office of the Superintendent of Securities
Consumer, Corporate and Insurance Services Division
Department of Justice and Public Safety
PO Box 2000
Charlottetown, PE C1A 7N8
Website: www.gov.pe.ca/securities/index.php3?lang=E

Saskatchewan Securities Commission
Suite 601, 1919 Saskatchewan Drive
Regina, SK S4P 4H2
Phone: 306-787-5645
Fax: 306-787-5899
Business hours: Monday to Friday, 8:00 AM to 5:00 PM

IDENTITY THEFT STATEMENT

[Note: this statement is to be filled out in addition to the usual RCMP victim impact statement. The Identity Theft Statement can be found at www.antifraudcentre.ca]

To: _____
(Name of financial institution, credit card issuer, or other company)

Part One: Information about You and the Incident

I, _____ , state as follows:
(name)

Personal Information

1) My full legal name is:

_____
(first)   (middle)   (last)

2) My commonly used name (if different from above) is:

_____
(first)   (middle)   (last)

3) My date of birth is (y/m/d): _____ / _____ / _____

4) My Address is:

_____

City: _____ Province/Territory: _____ Postal Code: _____

5) My home phone number is:_____

6) My business phone number is:_____

7) I prefer to be contacted at:
☐ Home
☐ Business
☐ Alternate number: _____

Name_____

Information about the Incident

Please check all that apply

8) I became aware of the incident through:

9) I did not authorize anyone to use my name or personal information to seek the money, credit, loans, goods or services described in this document.

10) I did not receive any benefit, money, goods or services as a result of the events described in this document.

11) My identification document(s), (for example, credit card, debit card, birth certificate, driver's licence, etc.), were:

☐ lost on or about (y/m/d) _____ / _____ / _____

☐ stolen on or about (y/m/d) _____ / _____ / _____

☐ never received

Additional information (e.g. which cards, circumstances):

12) Additional Comments (for example, a description of the incident, what information was used or how a possible identity thief gained access to your information):

Attach additional pages as necessary

This information notifies companies that an incident has occurred and it allows them to investigate your claim. Depending on the details of your case, each company may need to contact you with further questions.

Name_____

Investigation and Enforcement Information

13) I have reported the events described in this document to the police or other law enforcement agency.

The Police ☐ did ☐ did not complete a report.

In the event that you have contacted the police or other law enforcement agency, please complete the following:

_____   _____
Agency   Officer

_____   _____
Phone Number   Badge Number

_____   _____
Date of Report   Report number, if any

Documentation

Please indicate the supporting documentation you are able to provide. Attach legible copies (not originals) to this document.

14) A copy of the report completed by the Police or law enforcement agency. (if available)

15) Other supporting documentation: (Describe):

Part Two: Statement Of Unauthorized Account Activity

Complete this section separately for each company you are notifying.

As a result of the events described in the Identity Theft Statement (check all that apply):

☐ The account(s) described in the following table (e.g. deposit account, investment account, credit card account, etc.) was/were opened at your company in my name without my knowledge, authorization or consent, using my personal information or identifying documents.

☐ My account(s) described in the following table (e.g. deposit account, investment account, credit card account, etc.) was/were accessed, used or debited without my knowledge, authorization or consent, using my personal information or identifying documents.

The unauthorized activity took place through (if known):
   ☐ An in-person transaction
   ☐ An automated banking machine
   ☐ A point of sale purchase
   ☐ An Internet transaction
   ☐ A telephone transaction
   ☐ A cheque
   ☐ Other _____
   ☐ Don't know

☐ The credit product(s) described in the following table (e.g. loan, mortgage, line of credit) as/were obtained from your company in my name without my knowledge, authorization or consent, using my personal information or identifying documents.

Name_____

Description of Unauthorized Account Activity

Company Name/ Address	Type of Account/ Account Number	Description of unauthorized activity (if known)	Date (if known)	Amount (if known)

Attach additional pages as necessary

If the incident involved a **mortgage**, please indicate the following:

Lender's Name/ Address	Date of Registration (if known)	Legal description of the property	Municipal Address of the property	Registration Number of mortgage (if known)

Attach additional pages as necessary

☐ During the time of the incident(s) described above, I had the following account(s) opened with your company (please list any account not mentioned above):

Billing Name _____

Billing Address_____

Account/Card Number

_____

Attach additional pages as necessary

Protecting Your Privacy

I agree that companies to whom I provide the Identity Theft Statement may use the personal information in it only for the purposes of investigating the incident described in the Statement, prosecuting the person(s) responsible and preventing further fraud or theft.

The companies may disclose the information to law enforcement institutions or agencies (for example, police departments) for these purposes. The companies to whom I provide the Identity Theft Statement agree that this information may not be used or disclosed for any other purposes except as authorized by law. If this document or information contained in it is requested in a law enforcement proceeding (e.g. before a court or tribunal), the company may have to provide it or disclose it.

Signature

All statements made by me in this form are true and complete in every respect to the best of my knowledge and belief.

_____

Signature

_____

Printed name

_____

Date

Knowingly submitting false information in this Statement could subject you to criminal prosecution.

Notes on Sources

Information for stories throughout this text was retrieved from numerous sources, including several community news outlets, online and print publications, and special interest groups:

BBC News

bclocalnews.com

Canadian Anti-Fraud Centre

Canadian Business

Canadian Imperial Bank of Commerce

Canadian Marketing Association

Canadian Securities Administrators

CBC News

Consumer Protection BC

Criminal Intelligence Service Canada

CTV News

DailyFinance

Department of Justice Canada

Edmonton Journal

Edmonton Police Service

Equifax Canada

Financial Consumer Agency of Canada

Genworth Financial

Grey Power

Hackers on Planet Earth (HOPE)

Huffington Post

Investopedia

LifeLock (Identity Theft Protection)

National Do Not Call List

Office of the Privacy Commissioner of Canada
Ontario Securities Commission
Passport Canada
PC Magazine Digital Edition
PhysOrg (science, research and technology website)
Regina Police Service
Reuters Limited
Royal Canadian Mounted Police
Quebecor Media Inc. (QMI)
Snoopes.com
The Star
TransUnion Credit Bureau
USA Today
WAFF.com
Yahoo! Finance Canada

Book Sources

Arata, Michael J. Jr. *Identity Theft for Dummies.* Hoboken, NJ: Wiley Publishing, Inc., 2010.

Cairns, Alan. *Nothing Sacred: The Many Lives and Betrayals of Albert Walker.* Seal Books, Toronto, ON: McClelland-Bantam, Inc., 1998.

Hammond, Robert. *Identity Theft, How to Protect Your Most Valuable Asset.* Franklin Lakes, NJ: Career Press, 2003.

Holtzman, David H. *How to Survive Identity Theft, Regain Your Money, Credit, and Reputation.* F&W Media, Inc., Avon, MA: Adams Business, an imprint of Adams Media, 2010.

McWaters, Graham, and Gary Ford. *The Canadian Guide to Protecting Yourself from Identity Theft and Other Fraud.* Toronto, ON: Insomniac Press, 2007.

Lisa Wojna

Bestselling author Lisa Wojna has more than 26 non-fiction books to her credit, including three others with Quagmire Press: *Missing! The Disappeared, Lost or Abducted in Canada, Unsolved Murders of Canada* and *Canada's Most Wanted*. She has worked in the community newspaper industry as a writer and journalist and has travelled Canada from the windy prairies of Manitoba to northern British Columbia and even to the wilds of Africa. Although writing and photography have been a central part of her life for as long as she can remember, it's the people behind every story that are her motivation and give her the most fulfilment.